The Future of Latino Independent Media: A NALIP Sourcebook

Chon A. Noriega, editor

UCLA Chicano Studies Research Center
Los Angeles,California
2000

Library of Congress Cataloging-in-Publication Data

The Future of Latino independent media : a NALIP sourcebook /
Chon A. Noriega, editor.
     p. cm.
   Includes bibliographical references and index.
   ISBN 0-89551-096-0 (pbk.)
   1. Hispanic Americans and mass media. 2. Hispanic American
mass media.
   I. Noriega, Chon A., 1961-

P94.5.H58 F88 2000
302.23'089'68--dc21   00-37385

Cover design by William Morosi

U Chicano
C Studies
L Research
A Center
Publications
2307 Murphy Hall
Los Angeles, California 90095–1544 USA
aztlan@csrc.ucla.edu

Center Director: Guillermo E. Hernández
Publications Coordinator: Wendy Belcher
Business Manager: Lisa Liang
Journal Editor: Chon A. Noriega
Assistant Editor: Renee Moreno
Production: William Morosi

This book is a project of the

National Association of Latino Independent Producers (NALIP)
2822 Lyndale Avenue South
Minneapolis, MN 55408
612-874-2819
612-871-6927 (fax)
cac@intermediaarts.org

COORDINATOR

Bienvenida (Beni) Matias

STEERING COMMITTEE

Lillian Jiménez, Chair
Ray Santisteban, Vice-Chair
Chon A. Noriega, Treasurer
Rosalia Valencia, Secretary
Moctesuma Esparza, Executive Committee, Advocacy
    Committee (Co-Chair), Conference 2000 Co-Chair
Frances Negrón-Muntaner, Executive Committee,
    Conference 2000 Co-Chair
Rick Tejada-Flores
Ray Telles
Lisa Navarrete, National Council of La Raza
Josef Sanchez, National Latino Communications Center
Marlena Dermer, Latino Public Broadcasting
Felix Sanchez, National Hispanic Foundation for the Arts

COMMITTEE CHAIRS AND VOLUNTEERS NOT ON STEERING COMMITTEE

Bruce Baca, Communications Committee
Cynthia López, Fundraising Committee
Sandra M. Pérez, Advocacy Alternate
Fabiola Torres, Conference Program Coordinator
Ela Troyano, Advocacy Committee (Co-Chair)
Greg Gómez, Director, National Latino Arts, Education and
    Media Institute (California Non-Profit)
Jerry Velasco, President, Nosotros

CONTENTS

Editor's Acknowledgments

This book brings together material related to or concerning "The Future of Latino Independent Media: Public Television and Beyond" conference held in San Francisco, California, on June 3-6, 1999. That conference was presented by six convening groups: Coalition for Latino Programming on Public Broadcasting, Latino Producers Ad-Hoc Committee, Latino Public Broadcasting Project, National Hispanic Foundation for the Arts, National Latino Communications Center, National Council of La Raza. Cine Acción served as the host organization for the conference.

The conference resulted in the creation of the National Association of Latino Independent Producers (NALIP). A second conference is planned for July 6-9, 2000, in Miami Beach, Florida.

The following supporters made both the 1999 conference and this book publication possible: The Ford Foundation, The John D. and Catherine T. MacArthur Foundation, The Rockefeller Foundation, Screen Actors Guild, Continental Airlines, Anheuser-Busch Corporate Relations, National Council of La Raza, Corporation for Public Broadcasting, Nielsen Media Research, UCLA Office of the Chancellor - Academic Development, University of California Institute for Mexico and the United States (UC MEXUS), UCLA Department of Film and Television, UCLA Chicano Studies Research Center, UC-Berkeley Chicano Studies Program, KQED San Francisco, and KCET Los Angeles. NALIP thanks them for their generous support of the conference and its goals. NALIP further acknowledges the contributions of the following individuals: Lisa Baca-Sigala, Henry Cisneros, Fr. Virgilio Elizondo, Paul Espinosa, Natatcha Estebañez, Oscar Garza, Cheech Marin, Alyce Myatt, Gregory Nava, Harry P. Pachon, Raymund Paredes, Sandra Pérez, Peter Rodriguez, Rep. Lucille Roybal-Allard, Felix Sánchez, John Phillip Santos, Jimmy Smits, Peter Tortorici, Joan Shigekawa, Kathy Sosa, Jerry Velasco, Woodward Wickham, and Raul Yzaguirre.

NALIP is grateful to *Release Print,* the magazine of the Film Arts Foundation, and the Tomás Rivera Policy Institute for permission to reprint the following articles: "Missing in Action," "Talking Back to Television," "Rising from the Ashes," and "Learning the Hard Way."

The following people associated with the UCLA Chicano Studies Research Center were involved in the production of this book: Wendy Belcher, Publications Coordinator; Renee Moreno and Harry Gamboa Jr., Editorial Support; and William Morosi, Layout and Design.

Editor's Introduction

What a difference a year makes! On June 3-6, 1999, nearly 300 Latino producers and supporting individuals and institutions met in San Francisco, California. It was the first time Latino producers had come together as a national group since the civil rights era of the 1960s and 1970s. As such, it was the first time that most of the Latino producers in attendance had met face-to-face with their counterparts from around the country. That fact alone made the conference a success insofar as it laid the foundation for a national trade association, the National Association of Latino Independent Producers (NALIP). It also stimulated a number of bi-coastal collaborations as well as an active listserv for the younger producers just entering the field.

But the immediate crisis motivating that conference was that the Corporation for Public Broadcasting (CPB) had withheld Latino production monies for almost two years as part of a dispute with the National Latino Communications Center (NLCC). While there was strong disagreement among Latinos about the NLCC itself, the producers were united in struggling against a profound "disconnect" between CPB and a diverse and growing field of Latino producers. If CPB would not engage in a dialogue with the producers, then the producers would get together and talk to each other. While the conference remained very much a professional intervention organized by the Latino producers, they quickly established an open-door policy that reached out to all related Latino and non-Latino groups. That included NLCC. But it also included other groups that wanted to take its position, for example, the Latino Public Broadcasting Project (created by CPB in collaboration with Edward James Olmos) and the National Hispanic Foundation for the Arts. These groups agreed to invest time and money into the effort and to use the conference as a way to solicit input from the producer community. From the start, the National Council of La Raza provided crucial support and guidance. The producers insisted on an open-door policy, because they felt that backroom politics would no longer work: Latinos needed many media institutions, not just one; and they needed an open and transparent relationship with CPB, not bureaucratic paternalism. To its credit, CPB joined as both a sponsor and participant.

In many respects, this process put the crisis with CPB into a much broader context, explaining why so much was at stake for independent producers. Quite simply, since the 1980s, these producers have had few other places to turn in their efforts to make public interest and educational programs for a national audience. Despite the well-documented growth of the Latino community as a political and market force within the United States, Latinos have entered the twenty-first century with a lower level of media access and representation than when protests first raised the issue in the 1960s. As the *Hollywood Reporter* recently noted, "Hispanics have historically been the most underrepresented of all the minority groups in film and TV, and there is no sign that their numbers are increasing." In fact, guild figures released in late 1999 show significant *declines* from the previous year: from 4.0 percent to 3.5 percent for actors, and from 3.1 percent to 2.3 percent for directors. Latino writers for prime time television make up just 1.3 percent of positions.

But that's not the real bad news. While these numbers have remained almost constant for the last three decades, the Latino community itself has grown from 4.5 percent of the national population in 1970 to 11.5 percent in 2000. In other words, there are roughly two and half times more Latinos getting the same small percentage of the jobs. Think about it! Employment opportunity for Latino producers *as a group* has significantly declined to nearly one-third the level in the 1970s. Consider also that in Los Angeles, where the commercial film and television industry is located, Latinos make up around 45 percent of the population.

The fact that CPB monies had been withheld from Latino producers exacerbated their already limited access to media funding and distribution. For that reason, the conference was re-conceptualized from a town hall on CPB and NLCC into a broader event that would combine the town hall with both professional advocacy and project development. The conference included panels on documentary, feature, and new media production; but also included panels on the Latino market, audience development, advocacy and public policy, and SAG contracts. Finally, the conference provided a forum to meet with both non-profit funders *and* commercial buyers.

This broader perspective became the charge for the new group created at the conference. In the past year, NALIP has established working relationships with two major independent film markets—Independent Feature Film Market (IFFM) and International Film Financing Conference (IFFCON)—and two major independent membership groups—Association of Independent Video and Filmmakers (AIVF) and the Film Arts Foundation (FAF). And the planning for a second conference is already underway! Clearly, NALIP has a long way to go in terms of addressing the structural and situational impediments facing Latino independent producers, but it has hit the ground running.

Thus, if 1999 signaled an all-time low for minority representation on either side of the camera—best exemplified by the all-white casts for the twenty-six new primetime series scheduled for fall 1999—it also witnessed the first Latino national advocacy and policy efforts since the early 1970s. Other groups have joined the struggle alongside NALIP. The Tomás Rivera Policy Institute had already entered the fray in 1998 with a groundbreaking study of television. Throughout 1999, it conducted the first in-depth study of the Latino members of the Screen Actors Guild. In the months after the conference, the National Hispanic Media Coalition joined with numerous Latino civil rights groups to stage a "Brown Out" of the networks. By spring 2000—now collaborating with African American, Asian American, and Native American groups—the coalition had helped work out comprehensive agreements with the major television networks.

The need for a producers' group such as NALIP, however, is a profound one. Latino producers—as a professional group with defining characteristics and accomplishments—have almost no visibility within the press, the industry, and even the media advocacy groups fighting on their behalf. They are simply not part of the debate; and, hence, they are never identified as part of the solution. But these are precisely the people who will make the Latino images that are currently missing from our film and television culture.

Who are these producers and how did they become invisible in the debate over media representation?

Most Latino producers work in the area of "public interest" media, a term that has been used to refer to documentary, public affairs series, news programming, and socially relevant drama (shorts and features). Under the 1934 Communications Act, such programs satisfied the "public interest" standard applied to network television. In the 1960s, the "public interest" standard ushered in the Golden Age of the network documentary; in the 1970s, largely in response to a variety of social movements, it resulted in the heyday of local public affairs series. These series—which appeared on network, independent, and public television—provided the crucial training ground for a generation of women and minority independent filmmakers, including several who would later work in feature films. Since the 1980s, however, because of deregulation, public interest programming has become associated with public television alone. In other words, Latino independent producers became disconnected from commercial media at precisely that moment when it exploded.

Today, Latino producers operate in a fundamentally different media environment than was the case during the 1960s and 1970s. In June 1999, for example, PBS replaced *American Playhouse* with an anthology series for Hollywood talent to direct "the movies they always dreamed of" for public television. *American Playhouse* had been a major cornerstone of independent feature production in the 1980s and early 1990s. In short, the dreams of celebrities trump the needs of minority groups.

Oddly enough, there are many more opportunities than the 1970s, since film and television have been joined with cable, satellite, video, and digital media. Quite literally, there is about three times more work available! But while the playing field has both diversified and expanded, Latino producers find themselves excluded as much if not more than as in earlier decades. Latino producers find increasingly limited support through public television and non-profit or federal funding sources, even as these became their primary outlets. Meanwhile, these mostly independent producers remain outside the professional and corporate culture for cable, video, and new media operations that provide new outlets for social documentary and narrative.

We are in the midst of a digital revolution that has vastly expanded media outlets and the need for content, yet severely limited the number of access points to a handful of global media conglomerates. In the face of these changes, and the continued exclusion of Latinos, there is a need for many solutions, not one. Currently seven active Latino media groups take different approaches to this issue:

1. **Cine Acción**, founded in 1980, is a Latino media center based in San Francisco. In addition to its annual film festival and monthly film presentations, it provides such membership services as a newsletter, an information

clearinghouse, publicity consultation, and fundraising and production support.

2. **The National Hispanic Media Coalition (NHMC),** founded in 1987, is a media reform group that has filed nearly 100 petitions before the FCC in order to bring television and radio stations into compliance with the now-defunct Equal Employment Opportunity rule. Since the 1996 Telecommunication Act, NHMC has shifted strategy from FCC regulation per se and toward the political representation system. In fall 1999, it coordinated the Latino "Brown Out" boycott of network television, which represented the first such coordinated effort among Latino civil rights groups. Working with the Minority Media and Telecommunications Council, the Congressional Hispanic Caucus, and other minority groups, NHMC is involved in defining the viable advocacy strategies in the current regulatory and political arena.

3. **The National Latino Communications Center (NLCC),** founded in 1974, syndicated Latino-themed programming within public television. In 1998, the Corporation for Public Broadcasting (CPB) defunded its production grants program. The NLCC continues to operate a video distribution program and a significant film and television archive.

4. **The Latino Public Broadcasting Project (LPBP),** founded in 1998 and headed by actor Edward James Olmos, was created by CPB as an interim organization to replace the NLCC and disburse long-delayed production funds for Latino-themed projects. In 1999, CPB contracted the LPBP to continue as the official Latino consortium for public television.

5. **The Latino Entertainment Media Institute (LEMI),** founded in 1995, advocates on behalf of Latino producers, writers, and directors attempting to work within Hollywood. In addition to its trade publication *Latin Heat*, which provides in-depth information on commercial projects, LEMI hosts an annual entertainment industry conference.

6. **The National Hispanic Foundation for the Arts,** founded in 1997 by actors Jimmy Smits, Sonia Braga, and Esai Morales, offers graduate scholarships to Latino university students entering the five leading "pipeline" programs for film and the performing arts: Columbia University, New York University, University of Southern California, University of California at Los Angeles, and Yale University.

7. **The National Association of Latino Independent Producers (NALIP),** founded in 1999, represents over 250

Latino independent producers around the nation. In addition to an annual networking and trade conference, NALIP stages regional workshops and has developed working alliances with the major independent organizations and film markets. The NALIP conference in June 1999 represented the first such gathering of Latino producers in almost three decades, and brought together both non-profit funders and commercial media buyers.

These groups are either service- or advocacy-oriented. In one way or another each of the first six groups were involved in the steps leading up to the creation of NALIP. The common situation facing these groups is that Latino producers have been isolated from each other throughout the 1980s and 1990s and have thereby lost their potential power as an organized professional force. NALIP and its annual conference aim to change that situation.

For its part, this book brings together recent studies by the Tomás Rivera Policy Institute, critical essays by media scholars, and commentaries by emerging filmmakers and programmers. It also includes various conference reports and a complete directory of conference participants. This book is by its very nature an eclectic one that aims to put some useful information and individual viewpoints into as many hands as possible. It is a first step and something that we hope to repeat and refine with each conference. If anything, the directory alone proves the fact of our existence. The next time you hear an industry executive claim, "We looked for Latino producers, but could not find any," send them the book. How you deliver it, though, is up to you . . . .

Note

This introduction draws upon research the author conducted for a feasibility study for the Tomás Rivera Policy Institute.

Taking on Hollywood

Stereotyping and Resistance:
A Crash Course on Hollywood's Latino Imagery

Charles Ramírez Berg

The history of Latino images in U.S. cinema is in large measure a pageant of five basic stereotypes. Sometimes the stereotypes were combined, sometimes they were altered superficially, but their core defining—and demeaning—characteristics have remained consistent over more than a century and are still evident today. But there have also been exceptions to this rule: studio-made films that went against the stereotyping grain, stars who managed to portray Latinos with integrity despite a filmmaking system heavily reliant on stereotyping, and, more recently, a growing number of Latino filmmakers who began consciously breaking with the stereotyping paradigm of classical Hollywood.

This essay seeks to provide the reader with a broad overview of Latino images in U.S. film, delineating the main currents of representation—from gross stereotyping to resistance of different sorts. But to fully appreciate Hollywood's Latino imagery, in both its predominantly denigrating and occasionally more positive aspects, one needs to understand the narrative and cultural logic of Hollywood's filmmaking and storytelling paradigm, so we will begin there.

The Cultural and Narrative Dynamics of Hollywood Cinema

The stereotyping of U.S. Latinos and Latin Americans, and the defamatory stereotyping of many other socially marginalized groups (gays, Native Americans, African Americans, Asians and Asian Americans, the working class, the poor, immigrants, women), is largely a result of entrenched Hollywood storytelling conventions. If one of the distinguishing features of the Hollywood cinema is its goal-oriented protagonist, we can say with a high degree of certainty that, sociologically speaking, that goal-driven hero will be a white, handsome, middle-aged, upper middle-class, heterosexual, Protestant Anglo-Saxon male.

This great white hero is the sun around which the film narrative revolves, and the rationale of a typical Hollywood story is to demonstrate how moral, resourceful, brave, intelligent—in a word, *superior*—he is. It follows that the rest of the characters must necessarily be shown to be *inferior* in various ways and to varying degrees. In order to prop up the protagonist, characters of different cultural/ethnic/racial/class backgrounds from the hero are generally assigned sundry minor roles: villains, sidekicks, temptresses, the "other man." Their main function is to provide opportunities for the protagonist to display his absolute moral, physical, and intellectual preeminence.

In addition, we can schematically chart the standard Hollywood story in which this WASP male hero usually appears. Viewed strictly dramatically, it is a formulaic narrative that proceeds from equilibrium (a tranquil status quo) to disruption (a threat to the status quo) to the ultimate restoration of the status quo (the Hollywood happy ending). Looking at such a framework culturally, however, one sees it in a slightly different light. The status quo that is posited as the best of all worlds is one that is safe, peaceful, and prosperous all right, but also one that is upper-middle class, white, protestant, English-speaking—one that conforms to Anglo norms of beauty, and so forth. This WASP way of life is asserted as the norm, and this is what is fought for and must be regained if the film is to deliver its happy ending. In such a scheme, not only Latinos but all people of color represent an inherent threat to the status quo simply because they are markedly different from the established WASP norm.

The Five Latino Stereotypes

The five Latino stereotypes listed below exist within such a movie-making paradigm and are part of its story telling conventions. With that in mind, here is a brief rundown of the most commonly seen Latino stereotypes that have appeared in the first century of Hollywood cinema:

El Bandido. Most familiar is the Mexican bandit in countless Westerns and adventure films. His roots go back to the villains of the silent "greaser" films (*Broncho Billy and the Greaser* [1914]), but his appearance continues in a long list of Westerns and adventure films (for example, the two guides who betray Indiana Jones at the beginning of *Raiders of the Lost Ark* [1979] and the demented antagonist [Manuel Ojeda] who pursues Joan Wilder [Kathleen Turner] in *Romancing the Stone* [1984]). El bandido is dirty and unkempt, usually displaying an unshaven face, missing teeth, and disheveled, oily hair. Scars and scowls complete the easily recognizable image. Behaviorally, he is vicious, treacherous, shifty, and dishonest; psychologically, he is cruel, irrational, and overly emotional, quickly resorting to violence. His inability to speak English or his heavy Spanish accent is Hollywood's way of signaling his feeble intellect, a lack of brainpower that makes it impossible for him to plan or strategize successfully.

Though the Western genre is far past its heyday, el bandido lives on in contemporary Hollywood films in two incarnations. The first is the Latin American gangster/drug runner, such as Andy Garcia's sadistic Cuban-American gangster in *Eight Million Ways to Die* (1986), Al Pacino's mobster in *Scarface* (1983), and Joaquín de Almeida in both *Clear and Present Danger* (1994) and *Desperado* (1995). He is slicker of course, and he has traded in his black hat for a white suit, his tired horse for a glitzy car, but he is still compelled to satisfy his savage cravings—for money, power, and sexual pleasure—and routinely employs vicious and illegal means to obtain them.

A second *bandido* variant is the inner-city gang member seen in numerous urban thrillers and crime dramas. If the story takes place in New York, he is the volatile Puerto Rican (the toughs in *The Young Savages* [1961] and *Badge 373* [1973]); if in southern California, he is the East LA homeboy (the gang members in *Colors* [1988], the two hoods who taunt D-FENS [Michael Douglas] in *Falling Down* [1993]). What is important to note with both the drug runner and East LA Latino gangstas is that these newer images make only superficial changes to the external details of the stereotype; at their core, these characters are the same inarticulate, violent, and pathologically dangerous bandidos.

The Harlot. The corresponding female stereotype is a stock figure in the American cinema, particularly in Westerns. Like the bandit, she is a secondary character, lusty and hot-tempered. Doc Holliday's woman, Chihuahua (Linda Darnell), in John Ford's *My Darling Clementine* (1946) is an archetypal example of this type. Without a man, she is a leaf in the wind, so when Doc (Victor Mature) is out of town, she fixes her amorous attentions on Wyatt Earp (Henry Fonda). When Earp, decent WASP hero that he is, ignores her flirtations, she responds the only way she can—getting even by helping a card shark cheat Earp during a poker game.

A slave to her passions, the harlot's character is simplistically caused by her inherent nymphomania. In true stereotypical fashion, we are never provided with any deeper motivation for her actions—she is a sex machine innately lusting for a white male. A notable recent example is the character of Angelica (Jacqueline Obradors) in *Six Days, Seven Nights* (1998). She is the traveling companion of a small-time airplane pilot, Quinn Harris (Harrison Ford), and obviously romantically involved with him. But as soon as he is forced to leave her at an island resort on some business, she has no qualms about sleeping with the nearest available Anglo, Frank Martin (David Schwimmer). Angelica is an interesting example of a stereotyping blend, exhibiting characteristics of both the harlot and the female buffoon, and I will discuss her and the film in more detail below.

The Buffoon. The second banana comic relief, this stereotype can be of either sex. Classic male buffoons from television include Pancho in "The Cisco Kid," Sgt. Garcia in Walt Disney's "Zorro" series, Ricky Ricardo in "I Love Lucy," and in films, Leo Carrillo's characters in many of his roles in the 1930s. What is funny about this character, what audiences are given to laugh at, are the very characteristics that separate him from Hollywood's vision of the WASP American mainstream: his simplemindedness (the bumbling antics of Sgt. Garcia), his failure to master standard English ("Let's went, Cisco!" and "Lucy, you got some splainin' to do!"), his childish regression into emotionality (Ricky's explosions into Spanish).

In the 1980s, the Mexican comic actor and director Alfonso Arau (*Like Water for Chocolate* [1992]) played two roles based on this type: the romance-novel-reading Colombian gangster in *Romancing the Stone* (1983) and the bandit leader El Guapo in ¡*The Three Amigos!* (1986). It may be argued that these are parodies of the stereotype and, thus, healthy in breaking down stereotypes. But another view might be to question whether *any* use of such an oft-repeated and well-known stereotype can exist without in some ways serving to reinforce it. Are audiences laughing at the movie because of how cleverly it makes fun of Hollywood stereotyping? Or because it presents yet another ignorant Mexican who knows the word "plethora"? My guess is more the latter than the former.

The Female Buffoon is the comic counterpart to the male clown and, like the harlot, exemplifies a common way that the Hollywood narrative neutralizes the screen Latina's sexuality. This is a necessary requirement because the hero must have a reason to reject the Latina in favor of the Anglo woman and thereby maintain the WASP status quo. For that to occur, the Latina's sexual allure must somehow be negated. Generally, her character is smeared (she is made promiscuous and criminal, as is the case with the harlot stereotype) or ridiculed (portrayed as sexually "easy" or simply silly and comical, as with the female buffoon).

This is exactly what happens in *Six Days, Seven Nights*. The romance that Harrison Ford's scruffy and ultimately noble and heroic pilot has with the WASP leading lady, Robin Monroe (Anne Heche), perfectly conforms with Hollywood's storytelling and cultural purity logic. Once it has been demonstrated (to the audience, not to pilot Quinn since he and Robin are stranded on a deserted island) that Angelica, his Latin bombshell of a girlfriend, is promiscuous and has been unfaithful, he is morally off the hook and a free romantic agent. He can pursue a romance with Robin without the guilt of being unfaithful. Thus Angelica's sleeping with Frank, the secondary Anglo male character, is framed as casual sex and paints her as sexually frivolous. Quinn's falling for the WASP woman, Robin, however, is "more serious." It's one more illustration of Latino stereotypes being used to demonstrate the moral rectitude of Hollywood's WASP film heroes. Though Anglo heroes may stray and have sexual diversions with Latinas, they can still "redeem" themselves from this moral and racial transgression if they a) reject the Latina and b) are faithful in the "important" relationship—that is, the one involving an Anglo woman.

The antecedents to Angelica's female buffoon stretch back to the golden age of the studio system and is well illustrated by the striking Mexican actress Lupe Vélez, a comic star in

Hollywood from the late 1920s to the early 1940s. Best known for her role as the ditzy "Mexican Spitfire" in a series of eight films, she also starred in a number of other comedies. Vélez's Mexican Spitfire was an attractive dingbat, whose antics caused baroque plot complications that were not unraveled until the last reel.

Another well-known female buffoon is Carmen Miranda, who provided many colorful portrayals of Latin American women in numerous films in the 1940s. What is operative in Miranda's case is exaggeration to the point of caricature, another way to elicit derisive laughter and belittle the Latina Other. Miranda's multicolored costumes and fruit-covered hats donned to perform splashy "Latin" musical numbers (most notoriously, "The Lady in the Tutti-Frutti Hat" number from Busby Berkeley's *The Gang's All Here* [1943]) instantly mocked the folkloric costumes—and customs—of Latin America. This tradition of the exotic, comical, and oversexed show biz performer lives on with Angelica in *Six Days, Seven Nights*, a dancer whose Latin exoticism and eroticism are once again played for laughs.

The Latin Lover. This male stereotype we owe to one star: Rudolph Valentino. An Italian immigrant, by 1921 he had worked his way up from minor movie parts to a starring role as the protagonist in *The Four Horsemen of the Apocalypse* [1921], a story of the effect of World War I on young Argentinean men. In a famous scene, Valentino dances seductively with a cantina woman (again, the cantina harlot) and finishes by flinging her to the ground. With this and other film roles as the dashing and magnetic male Other (in *The Sheik* [1921], *Son of the Sheik* [1926], and as the rising bullfighter in *Blood and Sand* [1922]), he defined a new kind of screen lover. Valentino's smoldering presence in these films created the basis for the Latin Lover as the possessor of a primal sexuality that made him capable of making a sensuous but dangerous—and clearly non-WASP—brand of love.

Since then, the Latin Lover has been a continual screen character, played by a number of Latin actors, from Cesar Romero, Ricardo Montalbán, and Fernando Lamas to Antonio Banderas in films like *Never Talk to Strangers* (1995). All of these actors found themselves playing roles that Hollywood gave them to perform, reiterating as they did the erotic combination of characteristics instituted by Valentino—eroticism, exoticism, tenderness tinged with violence and danger, adding up to the promise that, sexually, things could very well get out of control.

Beyond the Latin Lothario character itself, however, there are less obvious residual effects of the stereotype. For example, in *Internal Affairs* (1990) straight-arrow cop Raymond Avila (Andy Garcia) investigates a crooked cop, Dennis Peck (Richard Gere). Somehow, Gere's bad cop intuitively knows he can manipulate Garcia by preying on his sexual pride by attacking his weak spot—his jealousy concerning his wife. Without explanation, and evidently based solely on the fact that Avila is Latino, Peck knows that Avila will become unhinged by his intimations about his wife's infidelity. And he's right—it works all too well. The implication: Latin males, even "good" ones, are different when it comes to sex; they are irrational and can't help it. Furthermore, Latin males will invariably regress to their basic bandido instincts, irrationality, and violence.

One more example: why did the screenwriter (Stu Silver) feel the need to make Mama's lover (at her Hawaiian home!) a *Mexican* gardener (played by Stu Silver) in *Throw Mama from the Train* (1987)? Presumably the gag lies in the fact that this stern matron would sexually let herself go in her advancing years with—what else?—a Latin gigolo.

Dark Lady. The female Latin Lover is virginal, inscrutable, aristocratic—and erotically appealing precisely because of these characteristics. Her cool distance is what makes her fascinating to Anglo males. In comparison with the Anglo woman, she is circumspect and aloof where her Anglo sister is direct and forthright, reserved where the Anglo female is boisterous, opaque where the Anglo woman is transparent. The characters that Mexican actress Dolores Del Río played in a number of Hollywood films in the 1930s and early 1940s exemplified this stereotype well. In both *Flying Down to Río* (1933) and *In Caliente* (1935), for example, she played fascinating Latin women who aroused the American leading men's amorous appetites the way no Anglo woman could.

A contemporary incarnation of the Dark Lady is María Conchita Alonso's character in *Colors* (1988), another stereotype blend. She is the Dark Lady for the first half of the film (where she is the love interest for Sean Penn's Anglo cop), then suddenly reverts to the harlot (when she becomes the mistress of one of the gang leaders to spite the cop and to demonstrate how little he understands the realities of the

9

barrio). According to Hollywood, then, beneath every Latino is a savage, a Latin Lover, or both and in every Latina heart is a Jezebel.

Bucking the Paradigm and Countering the Images

Although the vast majority of Hollywood films used these stereotypes when Latinos were portrayed, Hollywood cinema is not as simple, static or ideologically one-sided as *that*. Some films and filmmakers contested the simplifications of Hollywood's filmmaking conventions (and I'll discuss some Latino actors who resisted stereotyping in the next section). It's important to remember these films, not just out of fairness, but to recognize their creative courage, to counter the claim that it is impossible for Hollywood filmmaking to break with stereotypes, and perhaps to learn something about how stereotyping may be avoided. In the classical Hollywood cinema, Latino counter-stereotypes most often resulted from two kinds of filmmaking decisions: 1) in casting Latino actors to play Latinos, and 2) in the choice of ideologically oppositional subject matter.

In the first instance, without adopting the essentialist stance that holds that only members of a group can play that group, it is still true that standard Hollywood casting practice has most often had Anglo actors play Latinos, usually in brown face and complete with a thick Spanish accent (Eli Wallach's bandido in *The Magnificent Seven* [1959]; Robbie Benson's Emilio Mendez in *Walk Proud* [1979]). But striving for ethnic authenticity in casting not only makes sense in terms of realism, it often has a beneficial side effect on characterization too, allowing for a cultural shadings that might not have occurred otherwise. For example, in John Ford's *Fort Apache* (1948), the respected Mexican character actor Miguel Inclán plays Cochise, and he speaks Spanish and his *indio* dialect, bringing to his depiction a cultural resonance and authenticity that an Anglo actor would have been hard-pressed to provide.

The film also cast Pedro Armendáriz as Sgt. Beaufort, a Mexican American with a intriguing ethnic background. Once an officer in the Confederate army, he then acquits himself admirably as a capable frontier soldier. It amounts to probably the most interesting, complex and fully realized portrayal of a Chicano in any studio era film. Other memorable portrayals include Katy Jurado's Helen Ramírez in *High Noon* (1952) and Anthony Quinn's "Mex" in *The Ox-Bow Incident* (1943), two performances so rich in cultural texture that it's impossible to think of any other actors playing those roles. Lesser known but still impressive examples are found in *Crisis* (1950), the story of a couple (Cary Grant and Paula Raymond) caught up in a South American civil war. Director Richard Brooks made what could have been a cardboard view of Latin America three-dimensional by his inspired casting of Latinos in key roles: Puerto Rican-born José Ferrer as the egotistical dictator, silent film star Ramón Novarro as his chief military henchman, and Gilbert Roland as a rebel leader.

Films in the second, ideologically oppositional, category need not necessarily be radical in content or form; it is enough that they question the status quo, rather than blindly accepting it as perfect. A case in point is John Huston's *The Treasure of the Sierra Madre* (1948), which at first glance looks like nothing more than another Hollywood foray into stereotypical Mexico. After all, its lead bandit character, Gold Hat (Alfonso Bedoya), is the quintessential *bandido*, and he does deliver that classic line, "Badges, we don't need no stinkin' badges." But Huston's Mexico is more than simply a haven for bandits, and he depicts a broad sampling of Mexican society, from village administrators to Mexican *indios*, most of them (Robert Blake's shoeshine boy being the notable example) played by Mexicans who speak Spanish to one another.

Yet the film's most impressive counter-stereotyping aspect by far is its critique of U.S. imperialism in Mexico, beginning with the American oil company's exploitation of its workers. In this light, the quest of the three prospectors for gold becomes a cautionary tale condemning North American greed for Mexico's natural resources. In more recent cinema, there are the exposés of U.S. covert Latin American operations in Oliver Stone's *Salvador* (1986) and Roger Spottiswoode's *Under Fire* (1983).

Resisting the Stereotype

Throughout U.S. film history there have always been Latino actors who have resisted stereotyping, resisted as much as they could while being caught within the grip of Hollywood's

11

stereotypical filmmaking conventions. Lupe Vélez, for example, possessed a talent so vast it couldn't be completely contained by the Hollywood stereotyping machinery. In an early film like *The Gaucho* (1927), she puts in a great performance starring alongside Douglas Fairbanks. Her beauty and vivaciousness are matched by an athleticism that makes her the equal of the acrobatic Gaucho (Fairbanks). Though relegated to the B-movie side of the studio tracks by the end of her career, she single-handedly carried the tired Mexican Spitfire comedies with her sheer enthusiasm. Vélez is an example of an actor who is bigger than the stereotype.

Gilbert Roland, who evolved from a matinee idol in the late 1920s and early 1930s to a fine character actor, was another. His considerable screen presence bowled over stereotypes and replaced them with fleshed-out characters. In roles a lesser actor would have let slip into stereotype, like the Mexican rebel general in the Robert Mitchum vehicle *Bandido* (1956), he created a suave, smart, and self-assured military leader. And where the debunking of the stereotype was called for, as with the womanizing but insecure Latin star "Gaucho" in Vicente Minnelli's *The Bad and the Beautiful* (1952), he played the part with brio.

Another actor who defied stereotyping was Raul Julia, who never let himself be cornered into a type, even when it seemed there was no way out. In *Tequila Sunrise* (1988), for instance, he played the Mexican drug runner and deftly escaped the bandido stereotype by creating the most interesting character in the film. Sharp, witty, charming, and possessing a healthy, self-deprecating sense of humor, Julia played a fascinating rogue in the tradition of Orson Welles' Harry Lime in *The Third Man* (1949). And, like Welles in that film, Julia steals the picture from the rest of the cast, in this case superstars Mel Gibson, Michel Pfeiffer, and Kurt Russell.

Jennifer Lopez may be a contemporary example of an actor's persona overwhelming stereotypes. Though still early in her career, she has managed to steer clear of predictable stereotypes (save for the disastrous *U-Turn* [1997]). The most notable example thus far has been her portrayal of Terri Flores in *Anaconda* (1997), where she does for Latinas in action adventure films what Sigourney Weaver's Ripley did for women in science fiction in *Alien* (1980). Just as Weaver took command of a male genre and thereby forced viewers to reconceptualize it, so too Lopez is a modern-day Latina adventure heroine (following in the footsteps of Lupe Vélez's fearless woman in *The Gaucho*). With grit and perseverance Terri ultimately triumphs over the giant snake, while the handsome, virile Anglo lead, Dr. Steven Cale (Eric Stoltz), who would normally be the take-charge hero of such adventure films, lies unconscious for half the film. Her heroism therefore seriously undermines the entire genre's raison d'être: the ritual commemoration of WASP male heroism in hostile territory (and, ideologically, of U.S. imperialism in the Third World).

Obviously, the increasing presence of Latino filmmakers in the last two decades has also led to changes in Hollywood's stereotyping practices, but this topic is vast enough for its own article, if not a book. Suffice to say that one of the biggest challenges facing filmmakers of color today is how to enter the movie making mainstream without compromising their culture. Since, as a whole, Hollywood's treatment of Latinos has been largely though not entirely, stereotypical and since these degrading stereotypes are so intertwined with the type of stories Hollywood typically chooses to tell, it behooves any filmmaker, not just Latinos, to find creative ways to portray those on the social margins. For in the last analysis, breaking stereotypes is not just the morally responsible thing to do, it's smart filmmaking.

Missing in Action:
Latinos in and out of Hollywood

A Study by The Tomás Rivera Policy Institute

Harry P. Pachon, Louis DeSipio,
Rodolfo O. de la Garza, and Chon A. Noriega

Summary

The Latino/Hispanic subcommittee of the Screen Actors Guild brought a formal proposal to the Screen Actors Guild for a multiphase research project to investigate the challenges and concerns of Latino SAG members in the entertainment industry and to examine the Latino entertainment market. SAG, in turn, commissioned The Tomas Rivera Policy Institute (TRPI) to conduct the research and *Missing in Action: Latinos in and out of Hollywood* is the result.

A June 1998 Screen Actors Guild report determined that Latinos[1] are dramatically underrepresented on prime time television. They appear only 2.6 percent of the time during prime time and 3.7 percent on daytime serials, despite the fact that they comprise over 10 percent of the population. And they are much more likely to play minor rather than major parts.

TRPI scholars focused on a number of issues facing Latino actors and actresses in *Missing in Action*. They analyzed SAG data on the number of Hispanic actors and actresses, where they work, how many hours they work, what they earn, and what parts they play in productions. The scholars also held a series of round table discussions in Los Angeles, New York City, and Miami in order to talk directly with SAG actors and actresses and find out what they thought are the major issues they deal with in their work. The final part of the research for this report was a pilot telephone survey of the Hispanic movie-viewing audience in California. Coupled with data on the Latino entertainment market, TRPI surveyed 509 Latinos between the ages of 18 and 45 to determine Latino movie-going and television-viewing preferences in an initial attempt to determine the existence of a market for Hispanic-themed movies. A vast market remains largely untapped by Hollywood: Latinos, who are active consumers of the movies, television and video and represent a fast-growing audience with immense buying power. The key to reaching that market is already in the industry's hands: the national pool of Latino talent in front of the camera.

So far, Hollywood has had little information about Latinos' behavior or attitudes toward what they attend, watch, or rent. This study is intended to overcome this dearth of information and to establish a baseline for future studies. It provides hard evidence to support the arguments that Hispanic Screen Actors Guild (SAG) members have made all along: raising the profile of Latinos in Hollywood is simply good business.

SAG commissioned TRPI to conduct focus groups with SAG's Latino membership to assess the actors' attitudes about the employment and depiction of Latinos in the entertainment industry, and to come up with recommendations on how to improve the industry's ability to tap into this important community. SAG also asked TRPI to profile the Latino membership of SAG.

In order to frame these study results, TRPI also undertook an exploratory study of Latinos and their movie-going, video-renting, and television-viewing habits in California. Among TRPI's many findings, two stand out:

- The Latino audience for movies is split. U.S.-born Latinos are avid consumers of the movies, while foreign-born Latinos are less likely to see films in theaters (though a majority still go). Because foreign-born Latinos make up a significant share of the Latino community, the industry has a great opportunity to expand its audience. To build the movie-going audience, the industry must find the content and language in films that will appeal to this portion of the community, who in California make up over 50 percent of the Latino adult audience.

- Latinos are more likely to see films that star Latino actors or actresses than they are to see films that are equally popular but that do not star Latinos. While Latinos do not acknowledge the importance of ethnicity in their movie choices, there may be a relationship in the viewers' minds between films that star Latinos or focus on the Latino community and films that present Latinos in a positive light. While Latinos do not place ethnicity at the top of the list of reasons to see a film, it clearly plays a role.

Latinos are of a mixed mind about their image in movies and television. A slight majority report that Latinos are overall presented in a positive light. But they also report that the most common image of Latinos and Latinas is negative. Many also see stereotypes in the presentation of Latinos.

This attitude is mirrored in comments by Latino SAG members who participated in TRPI focus groups in Los Angeles, New York, and Miami. These Latino actors also said that they overwhelmingly feel that being Latino is an obstacle to their acting careers. As one respondent stated:

> I feel like there is a label that we have to get around, being "Hispanic." Behind what that word means, there are other presumptions that don't apply, aren't true and are false. Either we spend our time living up to those [presumptions] for the sake of getting a job, or we try and get around them.

In the context of these findings, the industry should be concerned that the TRPI profile of SAG shows that the number of Hispanics in SAG remains relatively low, at 4,852 members, compared with 73,358 non-Hispanic whites and 9,566 African Americans.

When asked what the industry and what SAG could do to bring about change, the Latino members were forthright and candid in their recommendations:

- Promote color-blind casting.
- Inform behind-the-camera decision-makers.
- Show the real American scene and increase Hispanic programming.
- Address pay and non-union work issues specific to Spanish-language TV.
- Have SAG play a more aggressive role in promoting Latino inclusiveness in the entertainment industry.

Note

1. We use the terms Latino and Hispanic interchangeably to refer to individuals who trace their origin or ancestry to the Spanish-speaking parts of Latin America or the Caribbean.

The Latino Community—a Huge Potential Market

Latinos are a movie-going community, an immense market for consumer goods and the fastest-growing segment of the U.S. population.

At the close of the 20th century, one out of five Americans trace their ancestry to non-European roots. And that number will continue to grow throughout the first decades of the twenty-first century.

Latinos make up the fastest growing and soon to be largest segment of that non-European population. In 1999 Latinos accounted for one out of nine Americans (see Figure 1). And due to immigration from Latin America and higher birth rates, this number will continue to increase. One generation from now—in the year 2020—one out of six Americans will be of Hispanic descent.

With this surge in population comes enormous buying power. National Latino buying power in 1997 was $332 billion annually, making the Latino consumer market the 14th largest consumer market in the world (see Figure 2).

Even though their annual per capita income is significantly less than the national average ($29,976 vs. $39,926), Latino families spend about 4 percent of their after-tax income on entertainment (e.g., movies, sporting events, family recreational activities), according to the Consumer Expenditure Survey (CES) of the U.S. Bureau of Labor Statistics. In the past four years for which data is available (1994-1997), Latino families increased their spending on entertainment by 20 percent, while entertainment spending by non-Hispanic white families increased only by 16 percent.

Latinos spend on average about $1,055 a year on entertainment (see Figure 3). While this is only 58 percent of what white non-Hispanic families spend, this figure represents an average of $200 more a year than what black families spend on entertainment. And Latino family entertainment expenditures seem to increase during good economic times. Latino families spent over $10 billion a year on entertainment in 1997! (see Figure 4).

On average annually, Latinos spend $74.28 per person per year on admissions (movies, concerts, theater, sporting

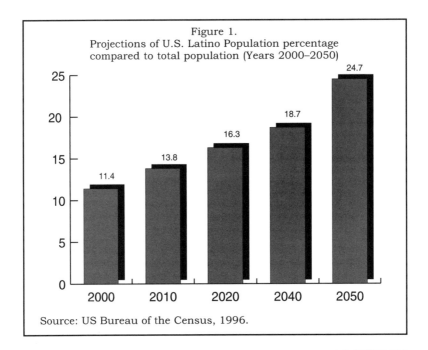

Figure 1.
Projections of U.S. Latino Population percentage
compared to total population (Years 2000–2050)

Source: US Bureau of the Census, 1996.

Figure 2.
A Comparison of the U.S. Latino
Market vs International Markets (1997)

Rank		GNP (Millions $)
1.	United States	6,137,367
2.	Japan	4,321,136
3.	Germany	2,075,452
4.	France	1,355,039
5.	Italy	1,101,258
6.	United Kingdom	1,069,457
7.	China	630,202
8.	Canada	569,949
9.	Brazil	536,309
10.	Spain	525,334
11.	Russia	392,496
12.	Mexico	368,679
13.	Korea, South	366,484
14.	**U.S. Latino Market**	**331,517**
15.	Netherlands	328,484

Source: TRPI analysis of data from The Illustrated Book of World
Rankings 1997 and the Current Population Reports, "Money
Income in the United States: 1997," September 1998.

Figure 3.
Hispanic, Black, & Non-Hispanic White
Family Entertainment Expenditures (1994–1997)

	Hispanic	Black	Non-Hispanic white
1994	$ 937	$767	$1,668
1995	1,058	926	1,701
1996	1,087	882	1,963
1997	1,137	872	1,940
Average Annual Expenditures			
(4 yrs)	1,055	862	1,818

Source: Data compiled by TRPI from U.S. Bureau of Labor
Statistics, National Consumer Expenditure Survey (1994–1997)

Figure 4.
Total Latino Family Expenditures
on Entertainment (1997)

Average Family Entertainment Expenditures
($1,137)

x

U.S. Latino Families
(8,905,000)

=

$10,124,985,000

Source: Data compiled by TRPI from U.S. Bureau of Labor
Statistics, National Consumer Expenditure Survey (1994–1997)

*Entertainment expenditures include movies, family recreation,
and attendance at sporting events.

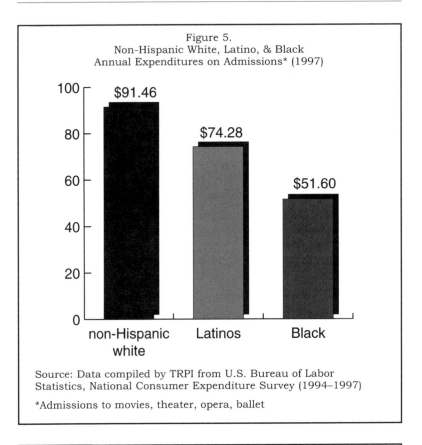

Figure 5.
Non-Hispanic White, Latino, & Black
Annual Expenditures on Admissions* (1997)

Source: Data compiled by TRPI from U.S. Bureau of Labor
Statistics, National Consumer Expenditure Survey (1994–1997)

*Admissions to movies, theater, opera, ballet

Figure 6.
Total Latino Family Annual
Expenditures on Admissions* (1997)

Average Family Entertainment Expenditures
($74.28)

x

U.S. Latino Families
(8,905,000)

=

$661,463,000

Source: Data compiled by TRPI from U.S. Bureau of Labor
Statistics, National Consumer Expenditure Survey (1994–1997)

*Movies, theater, opera, ballet

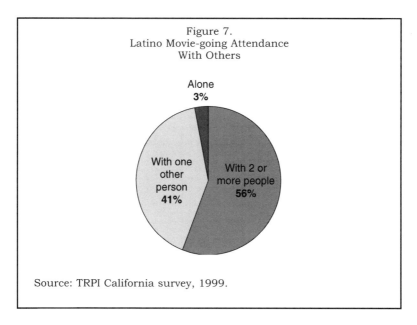

Figure 7.
Latino Movie-going Attendance
With Others

Source: TRPI California survey, 1999.

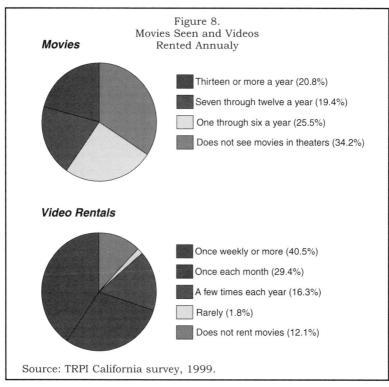

Figure 8.
Movies Seen and Videos
Rented Annualy

Source: TRPI California survey, 1999.

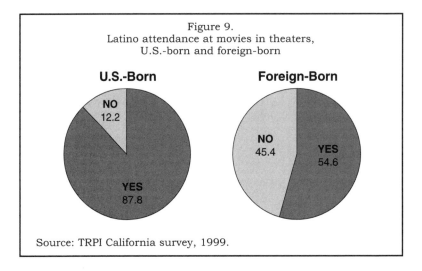

Figure 9.
Latino attendance at movies in theaters,
U.S.-born and foreign-born

U.S.-Born

NO
12.2

YES
87.8

Foreign-Born

NO
45.4

YES
54.6

Source: TRPI California survey, 1999.

events, country club memberships, opera and ballet), compared with $51.60 per person for blacks and $91.46 for whites (see Figure 5). If we assume that half of these admissions expenditures are for movies, the Latino community represents a $330-million annual movie admissions market (see Figure 6). In fact, if one looks at admissions as a percentage of overall entertainment expenditures, Latinos spend the largest share: they spend 6.5 percent of their entertainment income on admissions, while blacks spend 5.9 percent and whites spend 4.7 percent.

Movie-going patterns

In TRPI's survey of young adult California Latinos (18-45 years of age), two-thirds of respondents reported that they go to movies in theaters. Of those Latinos who go to the movies, many go frequently. Almost one-third of Latino movie-goers see a movie in a theater more than once a month. Moreover, they do not go to the movies alone. Over half (56 percent) go to the movies with two or more other people (see Figure 7). About 88 percent of respondents also reported that they rented movies to watch at home at least once in the last year, and 40 percent rent movies to watch at home at least once a week (see Figure 8).

However, not all Latinos are equally likely to go to the movies in theaters. U.S.-born Latinos—who make up approximately one-third of California Latinos between the ages of 18 and 40—are much more likely to attend movies in theaters than are Latinos who were born abroad[1] (see Figure 9). Among U.S.-born Latinos, almost 88 percent attend movies in theaters. Among the foreign-born, the rate of movie attendance drops to 55 percent. Although almost all Latinos rent movies, nativity also plays a role in that decision. Households with foreign-born respondents are almost twice as likely as households with U.S.-born respondents to report not having rented a movie in the past year.

The movie industry is missing a large potential audience: foreign-born Latinos who are much less likely to go to the movies than their U.S.-born counterparts. The movie industry should be concerned about the long-term loss of a potential audience because ongoing large-scale immigration guarantees a large population of recent immigrants with limited English skills for the foreseeable future.

Over one third (37 percent) of U.S.-born Latinos see 13 or more movies each year, or more than one per month. Over one in four (27 percent) of the foreign-born see that many movies. Slightly less than half (45 percent) of the foreign-born who do go to the movies, see only between one and six movies each year compared to 31 percent of the U.S.-born.

Interestingly, the foreign-born, for the most part, do not see movies in Spanish either. Only 10 percent (and 11 percent of the U.S.-born) have seen Spanish-language movies in theaters in the past year. These gaps in movie-going can be partly explained by linguistic differences. Approximately 63 percent of respondents who answered the questionnaire in Spanish reported that they could not understand English either very well or at all. These Spanish-exclusive Latinos were almost all immigrants, and many were recent arrivals.

The wide range of rental videos available in Spanish somewhat compensates for the linguistic gap in theatrical movie attendance. As already mentioned, 88 percent of Latinos rent movies at least once a year. While few respondents (approximately 4 percent) rent movies primarily or exclusively in Spanish, nearly one-third rent movies in both English and Spanish at roughly equal levels. The remaining 63 percent rent primarily or exclusively English movies. Renters of both English and Spanish movies are made up in large part of foreign-born Latinos who do not go to theaters. This behavior should concern producers of theatrical features. This audience has found that they don't have to go to theaters to see films.

Movie selection

A movie's casting and content do influence Latino movie-going behavior among a sizeable minority, though most Latino movie-goers say they are not the most important factors in deciding what movie to see.

Of those who reported going to movies in the theater, approximately 40 percent said they had gone to a movie in the past year because it had a Latino actor or Latina actress. Thirty-seven percent reported that they had gone to a movie in this same period because the movie was about the Latino community.

A similar pattern is repeated when Latinos are asked to identify their reasons for renting a specific video. Some 42 percent of respondents reported that they had rented a movie in the past year because it had a Latino actor or actress, and 40 percent reported that they had rented a movie because it featured the Latino community (see Figure 10).

It should be pointed out that, although Latinos like to see movies with Latino actors and actresses or films about the Latino community, they select films based more on subject matter than on ethnic considerations. When asked to identify the *single* most important reason for selecting a film to see in a theater, nearly one-third of survey respondents identified "liking that kind of film" as the most common reason. The next most common reason (offered by 14 percent of respondents) was publicity for the movie. When asked about the *most* important reason for selecting a film, few respondents said they based their decisions on explicitly ethnic considerations.

When respondents were asked about the *most* important factor in deciding which movie to rent, they again seldom cited ethnic factors. The single most important reason given for renting a film was "liking the story or subject matter" (35 percent). Next in importance was a good review from someone the respondent trusts (13 percent). Several questions in TRPI's survey demonstrate that Latinos are substantially more likely to see a movie with a Latino or Latina star than they are to see a similar movie that sold as many tickets, but that did not feature a Latino star.

In order to determine whether Latinos were more likely to attend movies with Latino or Latina stars, TRPI devised a test question which compared 1998's highest-grossing action-

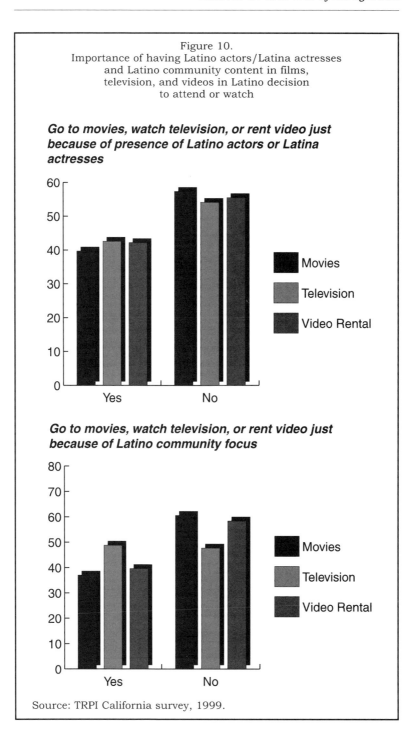

Figure 10.
Importance of having Latino actors/Latina actresses
and Latino community content in films,
television, and videos in Latino decision
to attend or watch

Go to movies, watch television, or rent video just because of presence of Latino actors or Latina actresses

Movies
Television
Video Rental

Yes   No

Go to movies, watch television, or rent video just because of Latino community focus

Movies
Television
Video Rental

Yes   No

Source: TRPI California survey, 1999.

adventure film with a male Latino actor, *The Mask of Zorro,* with a similar kind of film with similar box-office draw, but without a Latino star, *Enemy of the State.* We also compared the highest-grossing 1998 romantic-comedy film with a Latina actress, *There's Something About Mary,* with a similar, comparably successful film without a Latina actress, *You've Got Mail.* (see Figure 11) We also selected these four films since, at the time of the survey, these films had not yet been released on video. Because of this, we would only capture respondents' movie attendance behaviors.

Latinos who saw just one of these films were six times as likely to see *There's Something About Mary* than they were to see *You've Got Mail:* 36 percent had seen *Mary* and not *Mail,* while just 6 percent had seen *Mail* and not *Mary.* About half the respondents had seen neither film; 10 percent had seen both.

A more dramatic pattern appeared in the comparison between *The Mask of Zorro* and *Enemy of the State.* Latinos were seven times as likely to see the film with the Latino actor than the comparable film without a Latino star: 42 percent had seen *Zorro* and not *Enemy;* only 6 percent had seen *Enemy* and not *Zorro.* About 20 percent had seen both movies and 31 percent had seen neither.

Television-viewing patterns

TRPI also conducted a survey of California Latinos to find out about their television-watching habits. Those surveyed said they watch a lot of television in both Spanish and English. More than 95 percent of Latinos surveyed watch some television each day, and almost two-thirds watch between one and three hours daily. At the high end of daily viewership, 8 percent watch more than five hours daily.

Nearly half the respondents watch approximately equal amounts of English- and Spanish-language television (see Figure 12). Of those who watch more of one language than the other, a few more watch English-language television primarily or exclusively (31 percent) than watch Spanish-language television primarily or exclusively (21 percent). As we noted in an earlier study,[2] programming options are greater in English.

Children in Latino households are somewhat more likely to watch English-language television than are the adults. Again, approximately half watch equal amounts of Spanish and English television. Of those who watch primarily in one language,

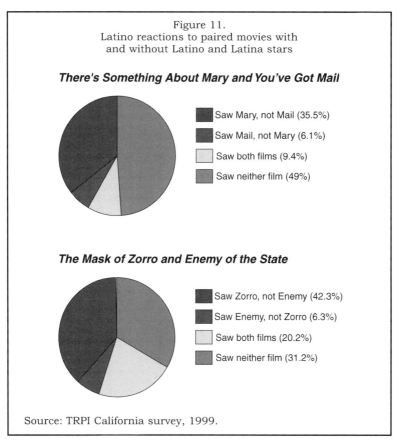

Figure 11.
Latino reactions to paired movies with
and without Latino and Latina stars

There's Something About Mary and You've Got Mail

Saw Mary, not Mail (35.5%)

Saw Mail, not Mary (6.1%)

Saw both films (9.4%)

Saw neither film (49%)

The Mask of Zorro and Enemy of the State

Saw Zorro, not Enemy (42.3%)

Saw Enemy, not Zorro (6.3%)

Saw both films (20.2%)

Saw neither film (31.2%)

Source: TRPI California survey, 1999.

almost all watch English television. Just 3 percent of the children in Latino household watch Spanish television primarily.

Almost half of the respondents reported that they have watched television programs in the past year because they featured Latino actors or actresses or because they focused on the Latino communities. Almost 43 percent reported watching a show because of Latino stars and 49 percent because the show focused on the Latino community. It's worth noting that these percentages are comparable, though slightly higher, than the answers to similar questions about choosing a movie or a video because of Latino stars or a Latino theme. It is remarkable, and supports our hunch that Latinos are drawn to Latino-based movies, that almost 90 percent of our sample had seen or rented *La Bamba* (see Figure 13).

Approximately 15 percent reported that they had purchased a product or become interested in one because the

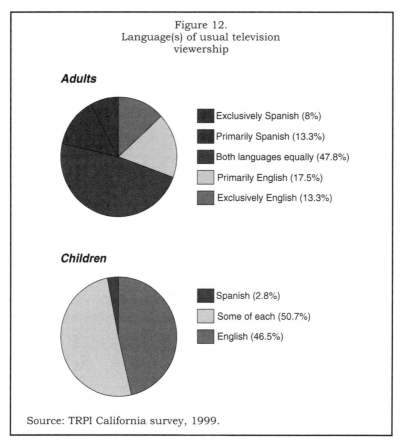

Figure 12.
Language(s) of usual television
viewership

Adults

- Exclusively Spanish (8%)
- Primarily Spanish (13.3%)
- Both languages equally (47.8%)
- Primarily English (17.5%)
- Exclusively English (13.3%)

Children

- Spanish (2.8%)
- Some of each (50.7%)
- English (46.5%)

Source: TRPI California survey, 1999.

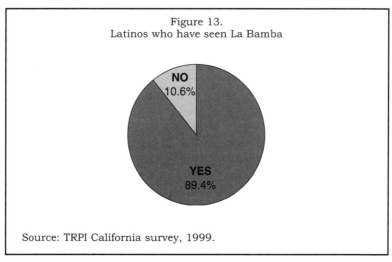

Figure 13.
Latinos who have seen La Bamba

NO
10.6%

YES
89.4%

Source: TRPI California survey, 1999.

advertiser had featured a Latino actor or used a Latino character in the ad. This finding may reflect the fact that most respondents did not report regularly seeing Latino characters in television commercials. Just 8 percent reported that Latino characters always appeared in ads. On the other hand, more than 51 percent of respondents reported that Latino characters rarely or never appeared in television commercials. The absence of Latinos in television commercials was observed more widely than in the movies and television.

Attitudes toward the portrayal of Latinos

Latinos reported that they generally don't see themselves portrayed in movies and television entertainment programs. While a slight majority of respondents report that Latinos overall are most often presented positively in movies and television, many respondents also reported that Latinos are often presented negatively.

Few respondents reported that Latinos were "always" present in movies and entertainment programs on television. Almost 47 percent, on the other hand, said that Latinos were "rarely" or "never" present.

When asked to identify the most common image of Latinos in movies and television, respondents distinguished between the images of men and women. Approximately 70 percent felt that the most common image for Latino men was negative: a criminal, a gang member or a drug dealer. For women, positive images were more common (though far from universal). Forty percent said that women were presented positively, compared to just 20 percent who reported that they were presented negatively. Approximately 10 percent said that women were most often presented as sex objects; another 10 percent reported that women were most often presented as maids or servants.

Despite these perceptions of the portrayal of Latinos on television and the movies, most respondents said that the overall presentation of Latinos was positive. Only 16 percent thought that overall Latinos were presented negatively and 34 percent reported that the overall presentation was neutral.

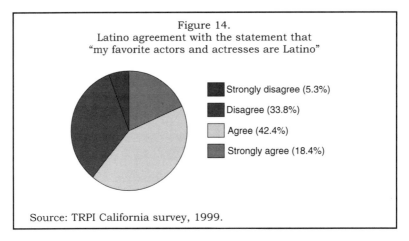

Figure 14.
Latino agreement with the statement that
"my favorite actors and actresses are Latino"

Strongly disagree (5.3%)
Disagree (33.8%)
Agree (42.4%)
Strongly agree (18.4%)

Source: TRPI California survey, 1999.

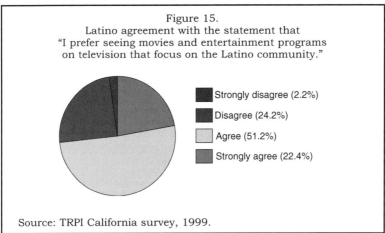

Figure 15.
Latino agreement with the statement that
"I prefer seeing movies and entertainment programs
on television that focus on the Latino community."

Strongly disagree (2.2%)
Disagree (24.2%)
Agree (51.2%)
Strongly agree (22.4%)

Source: TRPI California survey, 1999.

Latino preferences for movie and television content

Latinos prefer movies and television entertainment programs
that had Latino actors and Latino content. (These preferences
must be balanced by the seemingly contradictory findings presented earlier in this report that the majority of Latinos did *not*
attend or rent a film in the past year because a Latino starred
in the film or the film focused on the Latino community).

Over 60 percent of respondents strongly agreed or agreed
with the statement that their favorite actors on television and
in the movies were Latino (see Figure 14). Respondents also

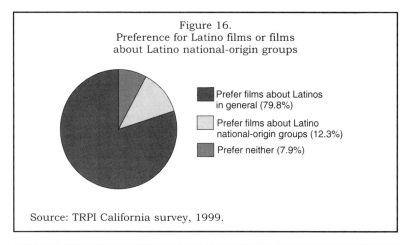

Figure 16.
Preference for Latino films or films
about Latino national-origin groups

Prefer films about Latinos in general (79.8%)

Prefer films about Latino national-origin groups (12.3%)

Prefer neither (7.9%)

Source: TRPI California survey, 1999.

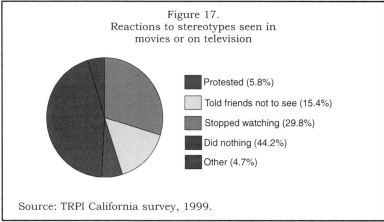

Figure 17.
Reactions to stereotypes seen in
movies or on television

Protested (5.8%)

Told friends not to see (15.4%)

Stopped watching (29.8%)

Did nothing (44.2%)

Other (4.7%)

Source: TRPI California survey, 1999.

agreed with statements that only Latino actors should play Latino roles. This position was held by over half of the respondents (depending on the question). Despite the belief that Latino roles should be limited to Latino actors, an overwhelming majority (89 percent) agreed or strongly agreed with the statement that Latino actors and actresses should be able to play any role.

Nearly three-quarters of respondents agreed or strongly agreed with the statement that they prefer seeing movies or television programs that focus on the Latino community (see Figure 15). When we probed respondents about what they meant by Latino content, nearly four in five reported that Latino content meant focusing on the Latino community broadly and not just on one Latino national-origin group (e.g. Mexican Americans) (see Figure 16).

The majority of respondents also reported that they liked movies about U.S. Latinos and about Latin America equally. While more than six in 10 liked both equally, 18 percent preferred movies about U.S. Latinos and 12 percent preferred movies about Latin America. Although the majority of respondents report that they have no preference between movies about Latin America and movies about Latinos, this finding should be balanced with the fact that only a minority (39 percent) has actually rented a film from Latin America within the past year.

Films, television, social harmony, and stereotypes

When asked for an overall evaluation of the role that movies and television entertainment programs play in American society, a slight majority (52 percent) reported that they built bridges between groups. One quarter felt that television and movies perpetuate stereotypes and 18 percent thought that they achieved some of each.

Finally, we asked respondents whether they had seen a movie or a television program in the past year that stereotyped Latinos. They were divided in their perceptions of the presence of stereotypes, with 40 percent reporting that they had seen a stereotype and 44 percent saying that they had not.

Of those who reported that they had seen a Latino stereotype, the majority acted in some manner to show their indignation. Nearly 30 percent stopped watching the movie or show; almost 6 percent protested; and over 15 percent told friends not to watch (see Figure 17). These findings, reinforcing the findings of earlier studies, demonstrate that there is a cost in perpetuating negative stereotypes of Latinos on television and in the movies.

SAG Members on
Being Latino in Hollywood

Given the ever growing Latino movie and television audience, how do Latino SAG members feel about being a Latino in Hollywood? TRPI conducted eight focus groups of SAG Latino actors in three cities—Los Angeles, New York and Miami—to find the answer.

Focus group participants said that being Latino is a two-edged sword. Although there was widespread expressions of ethnic pride in the rich, artistic heritage from Latin America in poetry, novels and theater, there was also a definite downside to being identified as "Latino." However, many expressed great optimism about the future growth and increasing clout of the Hispanic community.

Some SAG members shared one member's opinion that having a Latino surname "got me in through the door or because of your last name you get more specific calls for the Latin work." Others expressed the opinion that they had more opportunities since they could audition for Latino as well as non-Latino roles. Overwhelmingly, however, across the three cities, most SAG Latino respondents felt that being Latino was an obstacle in their acting careers.

The first of these perceived obstacles was the Latino surname itself. "They weed you out because you have Z's on the end of your name," one respondent said. Feelings were so strong that several respondents had changed their names to eliminate "sounding Latino" (as did Rita Hayworth and Raquel Welch). "I understand that my name has a lot to do with that. I have been told that my name is pigeon-holing me into the Latino market," said another respondent.

A Latino surname was not the only perceived obstacle. Latino SAG members said that having "a Latino look" could hinder or help their careers, depending on the circumstances. "Down here (Miami), they just come to find the Latin look," said one Miami Latino member. "They think that we are all the same." Added a Latina member from New York: "They told me I was too tan. I was told that I was too dark to put in the Hispanic file."

Accent and speech patterns can also affect employment, the members said. Curiously, it was the lack of an accent that caused problems for some SAG members. "I've lost out on work because I don't have a Spanish accent," said a Latino

New York member. Added a Latina member from Los Angeles: "It's hard to go after roles that are labeled 'Hispanic' because they want to hear an accent."

"I get prejudice . . . because I don't speak Spanish," said a Latino member from New York. "I finally learned that it is just a game. I had to learn to play the game. I got a job in a [fast food chain] commercial and didn't even have to speak Spanish. I got to look like me and talk like me. Didn't have to play a drug dealer to do it."

Typecasting was also a problem for respondents, despite the crossover success of such Latino actors as Andy Garcia, Cameron Diaz, Anthony Quinn, Ricardo Montalban and Jimmy Smits. "The system dictates that we are the prostitutes, maids, waitresses, gardeners, valet parkers—the 'bootie shakers,'" said a Latino member from Miami.

Added a Latino member from Los Angeles: "The director said, 'You know what? It is not necessary for you to audition. Let's not waste your time or my time. Obviously you are a person with culture and education, but what we are looking for is a Puerto Rican.' I said, 'I don't know if you realize what you just said is insulting. You're saying a Puerto Rican can't have an education and culture.'"

Once on the set, a minority of respondents recounted experiences with discrimination and ethnic slurs. "I was asked in a general casting call if I had my 'papers,'" said a Los Angeles Latino member. "I said, 'If you are asking me if I crossed under the fence last night in Tijuana, no. I've been doing this for twenty-some years.'" Added a Latina member from Los Angeles: "I went to sign a contract after I had gotten a role. The secretary said to me, 'Are you a real Mexican?'"

Latino SAG members across the three cities expressed the feelings that there was a "disconnect" between producers, writers and directors and the reality of the Latino community. According to Latino SAG members the entertainment industry continues to see the Latino community as predominantly poor, Spanish-speaking and of recent immigrant origin. This perspective, in their opinion, is further reinforced by the television news media and the demographics of Hollywood's Southern California location, where, according to Latino SAG members, the contact industry officials have with Latinos is limited to housekeepers, nannies, valets and restaurant help.

Moreover, Latino SAG members perceive that the industry has idealized a "middle America" audience that is not yet

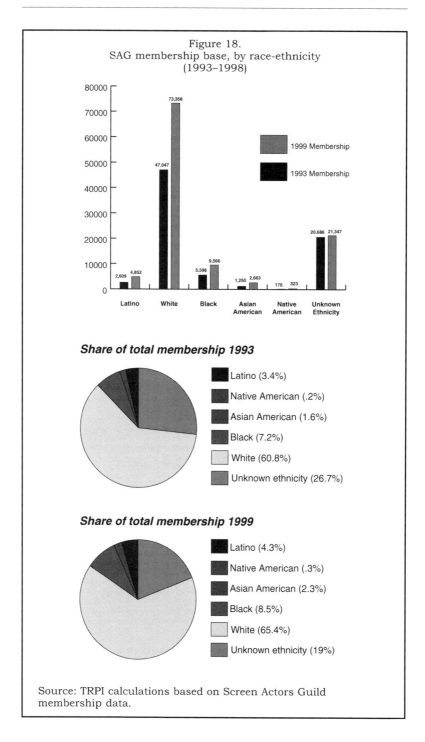

Figure 18.
SAG membership base, by race-ethnicity
(1993–1998)

Share of total membership 1993

Share of total membership 1999

Source: TRPI calculations based on Screen Actors Guild membership data.

ready for Latino characters in movies and television. The cliché, "How will it play in Peoria?" is alive and well in Hollywood, according to Latino SAG members. "I believe that there are ignorant casting directors," said a Latino member from New York. "They think that Latino is Puerto Rican. We have to educate them. That is part of the reason that we aren't getting anywhere." Added a Latina member from New York: "One-time shows seem to stay in the minds of producers, and that gives them a false sense of a Latino presence."

Latino SAG Members speak out

The following themes emerged from the confidential focus groups with Latino SAG members in Los Angeles, New York, and Miami. All quotes are actual statements by Latino SAG members and not from the authors of this report.

What it means to be identifiably Latino

> I feel like there is a label that we have to get around, being Hispanic. Behind what that word means there are other presumptions that don't apply, aren't true and are false. Either we spend our time living up to those (presumptions) for the sake of getting a job or we try and get around them.

What's in a name?

> I understand that my name has a lot to do with that. I have been told that my name is pigeon-holing me into the Latino market.

> In New York, my agent wanted me to change my name so that I wouldn't be typecast. I did. It afforded me the access to casting situations. It's amazing that the best part I've ever gotten in my life had to be in an Australian film playing a Latino.
>
> Latino SAG Member
> Los Angeles

The "Latin look"

> These casting directors called my manager and said, "We told you we wanted somebody who was Mexican. We wanted somebody dirty. He was white as far as we were concerned."
>
> Latino SAG Member
> Los Angeles

Every Mexican American has to be Eddie Olmos.
Every Puerto Rican has to look like Raul Julia. Every
Spaniard has to be Antonio Banderas.

> Latino SAG member
> Los Angeles

The role models (females) of the Latina community
are Jennifer Lopez, Daisy Fuentes, Elizabeth Peña,
and Salma Hayek. That's it.

> Latina SAG member
> Los Angeles

You don't sound like a Latino . . .

I've lost out on work because I don't have a Spanish accent.

> Latino SAG member
> New York

I was sent on a call as an "American mom" but they
said they thought I had an accent. I think because
of my name, it was a preconceived notion. I told
them, I do have an accent . . . a New York accent! I
either have to change my name or change my
accent!

> Latina SAG member
> Miami

I was very embarrassed when I was interviewed in
Spanish and answered in English. I'm just an
American.

> Latino SAG member
> Los Angeles

Crossing over and typecasting

I've played the full range of Hispanic roles...killers,
pimps, priests...

> Latino SAG member
> Los Angeles

I was building a lovely resume playing "Maria, the
Latina maid." It is very frustrating to not even be
considered for other roles.

> Latina SAG member
> Los Angeles

The last few years, I've had to play Colombian drug lords. I won't do it anymore!

> Latino SAG member
> Los Angeles

I've only gotten roles playing a nanny or house-keeper. There is prejudice but then even your agent is responsible for that.

> Latina SAG Member
> Los Angeles

Being Latino on the set

I usually have a problem with the catering service. They don't want to serve me.

> Latina SAG member
> Los Angeles

That catering service thing happens a lot. "You are an extra. You have to eat over there."

> Latino SAG member
> Los Angeles

Because I don't look Latino, generally I overhear comments about "those Latinos over there..."

> Latino SAG member
> Los Angeles

It's sad that we take these comments and say, "Gee, I'd rather not make a stink because I need the money."

> Latino SAG member
> Los Angeles

Why are Latinos invisible on the American screen scene?

I believe that there are ignorant casting directors. They think that Latino is Puerto Rican. We have to educate them. That is part of the reason that we aren't getting anywhere.

> Latino SAG member

The thing is that you are dealing with producers who are just interested in money. The say, "This is not going to sell in middle America."

> Latino SAG member
> New York

They have to open up and realize what America is right now. It is not what is being shown. The corporate world is not seeing it for what it is; they are seeing it from the height of their helicopters. There is an America that is not being reflected at any level.

Latino SAG member
Los Angeles

They either watch the news or all they know is their neighbor's maid or gardener. They assume every Hispanic person speaks with an accent.

Latino SAG member
Los Angeles

How can change be brought about?

Diversify to bring in Latinos to non-traditional Latin roles. Casting Latin actors for non-specific roles as the district attorney, the doctor, the day player. Then we would begin to see ourselves on television more. Then people would become accustomed to it. It would feel more like what our country looks like.

Latina SAG member
Los Angeles

Stop labeling "Caucasian male" or "Caucasian female." Leave it open. Let us compete on the same ground that Caucasian and even black actors get to.

Latino SAG member
Los Angeles

Why are we only called for the stereotypical Latino roles? Let us read. Open the doors so that at least a few people can be seen.

Latino SAG member
Miami

All I want is for it to be left up to my talent. I don't want to walk in and because you think I'm Hispanic, you think it's going to change the role or the fact that I can play the role.

Latino SAG member
Los Angeles

Educating decision makers behind the camera

They should look into including Latino writers in their projects. They should be invited to pursue them and let them see that there really are talented writers out there. I would encourage them to take advantage of the actors' programs that the WGA makes available to them. The WGA has negotiated access programs with all of the networks. They recommend, and they can only recommend, to the production companies that produce their shows to give Latino writers access, to give them a job, or to include them on their writing rosters. A lot of them haven't done it because it is *only* a recommendation.

Latino SAG member
Los Angeles

Somehow SAG must educate writers and producers as to what we (Latinos) are all about. They need to see our differences, our similarities and learn about writing Hispanic characters in order to make the character credible. Once that is accomplished, many other things will fall into place.

Latina SAG member
Miami

Maybe SAG could do some educational programming by giving them stats about consumers and the Latin dollar and population.

Latina SAG member
Los Angeles

I've never thought of myself as one of 30 million. I think of myself as an American citizen—who happened to come from Cuba. Hispanics in the U.S. are comprised of all kinds of nationalities and races! Can somebody PLEASE UNDERSTAND THAT!?!

Latina SAG member
Miami

We are very unrepresented in the production end in producing, directing and writing. It trickles down. There isn't a lot of flow because there isn't a lot of representation at those levels.

Latino SAG member
Los Angeles

Reflecting the face of America and increasing Hispanic programming

Networks have to take a chance on a Hispanic sitcom.

Latina SAG member

New York

[A cable network] is so afraid to even take a baby step in that direction. I'm only one actor. I can't change that.

Latino SAG member

New York

We want to see the happy, successful Latin family in television and film. The joy and wonders of the Latin culture have still not been touched.

Latina SAG member

Miami

We need to create positive images and images that show we are regular people. We might have a few cultural differences, but we work, we fall in love, we get married, we have children . . . I feel like in their eyes we don't live normal lives.

Latina SAG member

Los Angeles

Spanish TV and Spanish commercials

There are companies that run two commercials. The English version has SAG members and the Spanish commercial does NOT have SAG members. They can run that commercial for six years. That has to be stopped.

Latina SAG member

Miami

Get more union contracts on Spanish TV.

Latino SAG member

Los Angeles

If one corporation does union English commercials and non-union Spanish commercials, someone has to say, "You can't do that!"

Latina SAG member

Los Angeles

It's a SAG contract issue. [Spanish television] should be paying us more. That is something that has to be reworked as far as SAG is concerned.

Latino SAG member
Los Angeles

SAG's role

My recommendation is that SAG should have an annual meeting with the Latino membership to inform them of the Screen Actor's Guild policies and bylaws and contracts and any activity that the union is doing so that those members can be informed on what the union has to offer. They need to be informed on the Spanish contracts as to what they should get paid. It would be an informational meeting. Instead of only a few people knowing what is going on, the entire Latino SAG membership will know. They can be involved in the politics and administration of the union.

Latino SAG member
Los Angeles

Bitch and complain. SAG represents us! They need to do whatever [necessary]. This needs to be a focal point at their meetings. Advise as many Latino actors about the issues and what has been discussed and agreed upon.

Latina SAG member
Los Angeles

I think of SAG as a very powerful union, which is why I have felt protected and well represented. If SAG had a way of linking up a group of producers even within the Latino community, that would be helpful.

Latino SAG member
Los Angeles

We need to let the union be more aggressive in fighting for us. The casting agents don't want to be aggressive because they don't want to disturb the waters. We (actors) are not aggressive because we will lose work and will be blacklisted.

Latino SAG member
Miami

They need to make an effort to work with other
unions . . . to create an intra-union of Latinos. If
we can do that then we can have the [unity we've]
been talking about. Get the writers, actors and directors in a forum to work on constructive role
models. That becomes a strong base.

Latino SAG member
Los Angeles

A profile of Latino SAG members

The perceptions of Latino SAG members that participated
in the TRPI focus groups are confirmed when one looks at
the profile of Latino SAG members to discover what the data
shows about how they have been treated by the entertainment industry.

Latino membership in the Screen Actors Guild has boomed
over the past six years as all racial and ethnic groups have
seen their SAG membership grow (see Figure 18). But despite an 86 percent increase in the number of Latino members between 1993 and 1999, the Latino share of SAG has
increased only 0.9 percentage points to 4.3 percent.

In 1993, Latino members numbered 2,609 compared to
47,047 non-Hispanic whites and 5,596 blacks.[3] By 1999,
Latinos had increased their overall membership in SAG to

Figure 19.
Branch offices with more than 5 percent of
ethnic/racial group members

	Latino	Non-Hispanic White	Black	Asian American	Native American	Unknown Ethnicity
Los Angeles	57.6%	52.9%	52.6%	61.2%	65.3%	49.8%
New York	20.1%	23.6%	25.3%	16.7%	11.8%	29.4%
Florida	6.7%					
Hawaii				5.8%		
San Francisco				5.7%		
Total membership	4,852	73,358	9,566	2,663	323	21,347

Source: TRPI calculations based on Screen Actors Guild
membership data.

4,852. Whites had increased to 73,358, an increase of approximately 56 percent, and blacks had increased to 9,566, an increase of approximately 71 percent. The most substantial increase in this period was seen among Asian American actors, who increased their numbers by 113 percent to 2,663.

In terms of overall membership, whites continued to dominate the membership. In fact, their share increased from 60.8

Figure 20.
Share of Total Days Worked
By Race and Ethnicity, By Year 1993–1998*

	1993		1994	
	Total Worked	**% of Total**	**Total Worked**	**% of Total**
Asian/Pacific	4,460	1.8	5,484	2.1
Black	29,000	11.7	29,313	11.5
Non-Hispanic white	200,692	80.9	209,314	81.9
Latino	7,279	2.9	8,375	3.3
Native American	3,680	1.5	1,699	0.7
Other/Unknown	3,065	1.2	1,537	0.6
Total	**248,176**		**255,722**	

	1995		1996	
	Total Worked	**% of Total**	**Total Worked**	**% of Total**
Asian/Pacific	4,272	1.5	4,718	1.5
Black	33,498	11.9	42,738	13.4
Non-Hispanic white	227,168	81.0	256,527	80.1
Latino	10,148	3.6	11,643	3.6
Native American	1,977	0.7	1,274	0.4
Other/Unknown	3,291	1.2	3,203	1.0
Total	**280,374**		**320,109**	

	1997		1998*	
	Total Worked	**% of Total**	**Total Worked**	**% of Total**
Asian/Pacific	5,472	1.7	5,717	2.0
Black	40,561	12.9	35,794	12.6
Non-Hispanic white	251,920	80.1	230,078	81.1
Latino	11,641	3.7	8,226	2.9
Native American	1,373	0.4	696	0.2
Other/Unknown	3,364	1.1	3,236	1.1
Total	**314,353**		**283,788**	

Source: TRPI calculations based on Screen Actors Guild casting report data.

*1998 data are not for the complete year.

percent in 1993 to 65.4 percent in 1999. It should be noted that the share of Latino, black, Asian American, and Native American members also increased in this period, so the increase in the white share of the SAG membership results from the decline in members who did not state their racial or ethnic identity. Some of this change probably reflects the retirement of older actors who had never been asked to identify themselves by race or ethnicity and their replacement by new members of SAG who did identify their ethnicity. It may also reflect more complete data collection among members who had not previously identified their race or ethnicity.

Latino actors are slightly more geographically concentrated than other racial or ethnic groups, except Asian Americans (see Figure 19). Nearly 78 percent of Latino actors reside in Los Angeles or New York. An additional 7 percent reside in Florida. Among Asian American actors, slightly more than 89 percent reside in one of four regions—Los Angeles, New York, San Francisco or Hawaii. For other racial and ethnic groups, New York and Los Angeles are home to more than 75 percent of members, but the remainder is spread throughout the rest of the country.

Race and ethnicity in acting opportunities and roles among SAG members[4]

Latinos continually work less than their SAG memberships numbers would indicate (see Figure 20). In 1993, for example, Latinos made up 3.4 percent of the organization's membership, yet worked only 2.9 percent of the days worked overall in the industry. In early 1999, Latinos made up 4.3 percent of the membership, yet partial data for 1998[5] indicate that they again worked only 2.9 percent of the days worked by all SAG actors under union contracts. (It should be noted that although work days vary from year to year, with 1993 and the partial results from 1998 being the lowest, (see Figure 21.) Latino actors never worked more than 3.7 percent of days worked by actors under SAG contracts.)

Non-Hispanic white actors worked more than 80 percent in each of the years under study. Black actors accounted for the second highest share of days worked. Their share of days worked increased from approximately 12 percent per year in 1993, 1994 and 1995 to approximately 13 percent each year in the next three years. Asian American and Na-

Figure 21.
Year-to-Year Changes in Days Worked
Under SAG contract (all members)

93–94	+3.0%
94–95	+9.6%
95–96	+14.2%
96–97	-1.8%
97–98	Data not yet available

Source: TRPI calculations based on Screen Actors Guild casting report data.

Figure 22.
Days Worked by Lead or Supporting Role,
By Race and Ethnicity (1993–1998)

	1993 Lead/ Support		1994 Lead/ Support		1995 Lead/ Support	
	%	%	%	%	%	%
Asian/Pacific	37.1	62.9	43.4	56.6	47.8	52.2
Black	46.5	53.5	51.7	48.3	52.7	47.3
Non-Hispanic white	50.7	49.3	55.8	44.2	55.1	44.9
Latino	41.2	58.8	44.9	55.1	35.5	64.5
Native American	37.0	63.0	46.6	53.4	48.3	51.7
Unknown/Other	22.4	77.6	33.5	66.5	57.2	42.8

	1996 Lead/ Support		1997 Lead/ Support		1998* Lead/ Support	
	%	%	%	%	%	%
Asian/Pacific	42.5	57.5	33.0	67.0	40.9	59.1
Black	54.5	45.5	55.8	44.2	57.5	42.5
Non-Hispanic white	54.7	45.3	55.0	45.0	57.3	42.7
Latino	46.5	53.5	44.0	56.0	51.8	48.2
Native American	53.6	46.4	46.0	54.0	55.1	44.9
Unknown/Other	45.6	54.4	43.4	56.6	46.8	53.2

Source: TRPI calculations based on Screen Actors Guild casting report data.

*1998 data are not for the complete year.

tive American actors work a negligible amount of the total days worked each year.

Latinos are consistently more likely to be cast in supporting roles and less likely to be cast in leading roles than are black and white actors (see Figure 22). It should be noted that these designations are made by the production companies themselves and, as a result, might be inconsistent from one job to another and may overstate the number of actors in lead roles. Across the six years under study, Latino actors were cast as leading roles 44 percent of the days they worked. The comparable rates for white and black actors were 54.8 percent and 53.1 percent of the days worked, respectively.

Latinos and Asian American actors were more likely to be hired for daily roles than were white, black or Native American actors (see Figure 23). Of the days worked by Asian American actors in the six years under study, 61.2 percent were employed on daily contracts. The comparable rates for Latino actors were 55.7 percent of days worked. Less than half of the days worked by whites, blacks and Native Americans were for daily contracts—49.3 percent, 45.0 percent, and 45.5 percent respectively. These, of course, are averages. As a result, they mask some variation across the specific years under study.

At the other extreme, white actors are considerably more likely than any of the other racial and ethnic populations to be hired for series work. Of the days worked by white actors in the six years under study, slightly more than 30 percent were employed for an entire series. Just 25 percent of the days worked by black actors went to series work. Latinos, Native Americans, and Asian Americans saw an even lower share of their days worked going to series work—18.7 percent, 15.9 percent, and 10.9 percent, respectively.

Earnings[6]

The widely varying opportunities for work translate into disparities in the average earnings levels for SAG members of different racial and ethnic groups (see Figure 24). In all cases these averages are low and give credence to the stereotype of the starving actor who holds other jobs to survive. But it is important to note that even in this profession where many earn very little, there is variation in average earnings by racial and ethnic group. The ethnic and racial groups that are

Figure 23.
Percentage of Hires, By Racial or
Ethnic Group, by Type of Hire (1993–1998)

	1993 Daily/ Weekly/ Series			1994 Daily/ Weekly/ Series			1995 Daily/ Weekly/ Series		
	%	%	%	%	%	%	%	%	%
Asian/Pacific	63.7	30.2	6.1	60.0	26.2	13.9	58.6	28.3	13.1
Black	48.4	23.3	28.3	44.3	24.6	31.1	46.2	26.4	27.4
Non-Hispanic white	50.1	26.0	23.9	46.4	25.9	27.8	48.7	27.7	23.6
Latino	55.5	22.6	22.0	55.8	24.8	19.4	59.2	29.8	11.0
Native American	45.3	35.9	18.9	47.5	27.5	25.0	45.1	47.7	8.3
Unknown/Other	72.3	27.4	0.4	75.3	20.0	4.8	55.5	23.2	21.3

	1996 Daily/ Weekly/ Series			1997 Daily/ Weekly/ Series			1998* Daily/ Weekly/ Series		
	%	%	%	%	%	%	%	%	%
Asian/Pacific	64.7	23.1	13.1	63.1	31.9	5.0	57.3	28.7	14.0
Black	44.7	25.1	30.1	42.4	25.8	31.9	44.0	23.2	32.7
Non-Hispanic white	48.4	26.6	25.0	50.8	25.1	24.1	51.5	24.6	23.9
Latino	54.2	26.0	19.8	52.9	27.5	19.6	56.3	23.2	20.5
Native American	46.8	42.2	11.0	44.4	41.5	14.1	44.1	37.8	18.1
Unknown/Other	62.9	21.0	16.0	65.9	28.3	5.7	62.6	29.0	8.4

Source: TRPI calculations based on Screen Actors Guild casting
report data.
*1998 data are not for the complete year.

Figure 24.
Average Earnings of SAG Members,
by Race and Ethnicity (1993 and 1997)

	1993 All Members	1997 All Members	1997 Members with Earnings
	Average	Average	Average
Non-Hispanic white	$11,725	$13,103	$13,623
African American	$12,239	$15,727	$16,272
Latino	$9,101	$10,841	$11,328
Asian American	$7,396	$8,684	$9,193
Native American	$18,688	$9,211	$9,534

Source: TRPI calculations based on Screen Actors Guild pension data.
This table excludes the earnings of SAG members for whom there is
no record of the member's race or ethnicity.
1997 is the last year for which there are complete data.

most likely to be cast in leading roles and employed for weekly and series commitments earn higher average salaries.

In 1993, for example, the average Asian American SAG member earned just $7,396 while the average Native American earned $18,688. Black and white members earned at average levels in between these extremes—$12,239 and $11,725, respectively. The average earnings of Latino SAG members were closer to the levels of Asian Americans than to those of the other groups, at $9,101.

The differences between the average income by racial or ethnic group have narrowed somewhat since 1993. Asian Americans continued to have the lowest average income, at $8,684. At the other extreme, the average black actor earned $15,727. The average Latino continued to be nearer to the lowest than the highest average annual income, at $10,841. When the 3,027 SAG members for whom there are racial and ethnic data but who had no income in 1997, are excluded from the analysis, average incomes among working actors and actresses increased by approximately 4 percent.

Clearly, these average incomes mask a great disparity in incomes within each racial and ethnic group. Some highly publicized stars earn 20 million dollars for a single film while others show small incomes for residuals for a brief screen appearance many years earlier. The SAG pension system, on which these data are based, excludes some earnings from high-earning stars who are not required by the union contract to record all their theatrical fees for pension purposes. The SAG membership includes many members of other theatrical unions whose income includes SAG-covered productions as well as productions covered by other unions' contracts.

Policy recommendations

As Hollywood enters the twenty-first century, it will be forced to confront the changing American scene for economic reasons if nothing more. Hispanics are a fast-growing segment of the audience for movies, television and home video. But the industry is still not reaching all of its potential Hispanic audience.

When asked what the industry and what SAG could do to bring about change, Latino SAG members were forthright and candid in their recommendations:

Promote color-blind casting. SAG Latino members adamantly urged the industry to allow Latinos to be seen in the full gamut of roles that Latinos now play in American society— from teachers to lawyers, from physicians to soldiers, from soccer moms to nurses. As one veteran Latino SAG member put it, "Stop pigeon-holing Latino actors into the Latino file.

Inform decision-makers behind the cameras. SAG Latino members felt that the gap between creative personnel, decision-makers and the Latino community needs to be bridged. This will require a substantive commitment from both SAG and the industry as well as community groups. At each of the SAG focus groups members noted that the Latino community did not yet have an organization like the black community's NAACP or a national figure like Jesse Jackson pressuring the industry to educate and police itself. Specifically mentioned was the need to educate writers or to bring in Latino writers who would portray more credible Latino characters. They also suggested setting up mentorship programs for Latino actors who want to go into directing or producing. Latino SAG members also cited a need for Latino venture capital to finance Latino productions.

Show the real American scene and increase Hispanic programming. SAG Latino members vehemently expressed the need for the industry to more accurately reflect the face of America, and felt that SAG should hold the industry accountable. One SAG member felt that the lack of Hispanic faces in positive role models was a "crime. [Look] what it's doing to our Hispanic youth." Recommendations ranged from insuring that background actors reflect the true diversity of cities like Los Angeles or New York, to encouraging networks to take a chance on a Latino sitcom.

Address pay issues and non-union work especially related to Spanish-language TV. SAG Latino members said they were very dissatisfied over the low pay scales on Spanish TV and for Spanish commercials. They said they thought SAG needed to clarify and justify the existence of a two-tiered system of pay for Spanish- and English-language commercials. They were very concerned that SAG was "not doing enough" about non-union hires and productions by Spanish-language television networks in cities like Tijuana, Mexico.

Have SAG play a more aggressive role in promoting Latino inclusiveness in the entertainment industry. SAG members do not know about the efforts SAG is undertaking to promote Latino inclusiveness in the industry. Members in all three cities clearly called on SAG to work harder at linking producers with Latino actors and ensuring that Latinos are represented accurately on the screen. SAG should also take steps to inform the Latino SAG membership about its activities in this area. SAG should institute programs that recognize producers and programs that portray Latinos in a positive light. Conversely, SAG should meet with producers and directors who produce the most egregious stereotypes. SAG should also establish a confidential hotline that Latino and other minority actors could call to report casting directors who ask for the performer's ethnicity during auditions.

Conclusion

Latinos are avid consumers of movies, television and video, are the fastest-growing segment of the population, represent massive buying power and are an untapped resource for the entertainment industry.

Findings of this study show that the industry has an opportunity to capitalize on this important market by increasing the representation of Latino and Latina actors in productions; mounting more projects keyed to the Latino community and Latino themes; and being sensitive to its portrayals of Latinos in all of its work.

Latinos, as has been shown, are not an uncritical audience. To keep the present generation of moviegoers coming to the theaters and television-watchers viewing television—as well as to reach out to new audiences—the entertainment industry must pay attention the concerns raised in this study. As Latinos become a larger share of the national audience, their preferences will increasingly shape the success or failure of the entertainment industry.

Notes

Commissioned by Screen Actors Guild. Made possible by a grant from SAG–Producers Industry Advancement and Cooperative Fund.

The authors would like to acknowledge the assistance of the many people who made this research project and report possible. We would especially like to thank Richard Masur, president of the Screen Actors Guild, and Patricia Heisser Metoyer, Ph.D., executive administrator of the Affirmative Action Department, for their help withi this project. We would also like to gratefully acknowledge the active involvement of members of the Latino/Hispanic Subcommittee of SAG who provided their support every step of the way and the many Latino SAG members who gave generously of their time.

This project would not have been possible without the help of Karen Escalante-Dalton, TRPI vice president of operations who, at every stage of the project, provided a sounding board for ideas and concerns, and ensured that the report would be produced.

This study was made possible through funding from SAG–Producers Industry Advancement and Cooperative Fund. TRPI received supplemental support from Anheuser Busch which funded the survey component of California movie-goers and video-watchers.

1. For the purposes of this analysis, we treat the few native Puerto Ricans in the survey as foreign-born. Puerto Ricans are U.S. citizens by birth and, hence, are U.S.-born. In previous analysis, however, we have found that their behaviors in terms of television are more like those of the foreign-born than the U.S.-born and, so, we treat them here as "foreign-born.".

2. *Talking Back to Television: Latinos Discuss How Television Portrays Them and the Quality of Programming Options.* September 1998. The Tomás Rivera Policy Institute, Claremont, Calif.

3. SAG does not maintain race and ethnicity data on all members. In 1993, 20,686 had not reported their race or ethnicity, making up approximately 27 percent of members. By 1998, the members with no racial or ethnic identifier had increased slightly to 21,347. Due to the dramatic increase in membership, these non-ethnically identified members made up a smaller share of the overall membership—19.0 percent.

4. Data in this section is derived by TRPI analysis of Casting Data Reports submitted by SAG contract productions to SAG. Although required by the contract, there is little enforcement of the submission requirement and no verification of the accuracy of these reports.

5. At this writing, SAG has not compiled complete casting report data for 1998. Although we do not yet have a final measure of the number of days worked overall in 1998, the figures that we report here represent approximately 90 percent of the number of days worked in 1996 and 1997, suggesting that these data are nearly complete.

6. These data are calculated based on SAG pension records.

7. We use the terms Latino and Hispanic interchangeably to refer to individuals who trace their origin or ancestry to the Spanish-speaking nations of Latin America or the Caribbean.

Sources Cited

Tomás Rivera Policy Institute. 1998. *Talking Back to Television: Latinos Discuss How Television Portrays Them and the Quality of Programming Options.* Claremont, CA: Tomás Rivera Policy Institute.

Tomás Rivera Policy Institute. 1999. *Engaging Television in English y en Español.* Claremont, CA: Tomás Rivera Policy Institute.

Appendix

Methodology

In an effort to measure how Latinos engaged television and film and how they reacted to their portrayals in those media, the Tomás Rivera Policy Institute undertook an exploratory study of Latinos. Our study sought to establish baseline data on Latino film going, television viewing, film rental, and attitudes toward the images of Latinos presented in these media. As there is little research publicly available on these questions, we undertook this study with twin objectives. First, we wanted to ascertain whether such a survey could be successfully undertaken among Latino communities prior to conducting such a survey nationwide. Second, we wanted measure the connections between audience perceptions of the products of the film and television industries and the perceptions of Screen Actors Guild (SAG) members measured through the focus groups reported on elsewhere in this report.

We should acknowledge that the results of this survey should be interpreted rather narrowly. Although the sample size is quite large for a study such as this—509 respondents, this study was narrowly targeted to California Latino adults of the ages most likely to see films and who are most sought out by the film and television industry. Our respondents were all between the ages of 18 and 40. Thus, we can only hypothesize about the behaviors and attitudes of older Latinos and of Latinos outside of California. That said, the survey allows us to identify several important patterns of interaction between Latinos and the visual arts that we did not previously know. Further, the results are baseline data that allow for more rigorous comparisons when further studies are conducted of older Latinos or of Latinos in states other than California. Finally, we were able to see that the Latino film-going audience is somewhat divided along nativity lines, with the U.S.-born generally more engaged in film and the foreign-born less so.

The survey was conducted by telephone during March 1999 from a statewide telephone list of households with Spanish-surnamed members. The average survey took 13 minutes to complete. All interviewers were fully bilingual and slightly less than two-thirds of respondents chose to be interviewed in Spanish. A discussion of the demographic characteristics of the sample is presented at the end of this report, though it is important to remember throughout that our respondents are all between the ages of 18 and 40 and are all from California.

Sample Characteristics

The survey consisted of 509 respondents from California. A survey of this size has a 4.4 percent margin of error for questions that were answered by all or most respondents to the survey. A margin of error of this magnitude means that there is a high (95 percent) probability that the answers that we would receive if we asked all Latinos between the ages of 18 and 40 these questions are within 4.4 percent (either high or low) of the answers presented here.

All respondents resided in households with a Spanish-surnamed householder and self-identified as Latino. This sample is relatively unique, so it is important to examine the demographic characteristics of survey respondents to get a sense of the types of people who were answering survey questions. It should be noted that the sample is broadly representative of California Latinos between the ages of 18 and 40.

A slight majority (51 percent) was women. Three-quarters of households had children under 18 in the household. Household incomes tended to be low, though this might be in part a result of limiting the respondent pool to individuals between 18 and 40 (thus excluding households with one or two older workers with commensurately higher incomes and no young adults). Among respondents who provided household incomes, the average fell between $10,000 and $20,000. Just 14 percent of respondents had household incomes exceeding $40,000 annually. Approximately 20 percent of respondents refused to provide information on household incomes. The average respondent had completed 12 years of education and had earned a high school degree. Considering that this is a younger than average population, these education levels are broadly representative of Latinos in California. Slightly more than 18 percent had earned a post-high school degree.

We limited the respondent pool to Latinos between the ages of 18 and 40 in order to target respondents who were the most likely to attend movies on a regular basis. As a result, the average age of respondents was 29.

Approximately one-third of respondents was born in the United States. More than four in five of these U.S.-born respondents trace their ancestry to Mexico. Among the foreign-born, which made up two-thirds of respondents, Mexico was by far the most common place of birth. Respondents born in Central America made up approximately ten percent of respondents. The average foreign-born respondent had resided in the United States for approximately 12 years.

This nativity data explains a final characteristic of the sample. Approximately 64 percent completed the questionnaire in Spanish. Of these Spanish speakers, approximately 63 percent report that they cannot understand English very well or at all. It is this audience, with weak English-language abilities, that does not see films in English. Among the respondents who answered the questionnaire in English, fully three in four reports that they can understand Spanish, either well or very well.

Methodology for SAG Focus Groups

The Tomás Rivera Policy Institute research team conducted seven focus groups with Latino SAG members: four in Los Angeles, two in New York and one in Miami during February and March 1999. An average of twelve participants attended each group session. Participants ranged in age and in countries of origin. SAG participants were asked a series of industry-related and occupational-experience questions. Confidentiality of attribution was assured. In addition, individual interviews were held with higher visibility SAG members and members of the Writer's Guild. The following themes emerged from the group sessions and individual interviews. All quotes are actual statements by Latino SAG members and not from the authors of this report.

Talking Back to Television:

Latinos Discuss How Television Portrays Them and the Quality of Programming Options

A Study by The Tomás Rivera Policy Institute

Louis DeSipio with Sarah Banet-Weiser,
Karen Escalante-Dalton, and Federico Subervi-Vélez

Summary

Latinos represent an increasing share of the television audience nationwide and have been shown by previous studies to be avid viewers of television. Yet, there is no national survey data that reports how Latinos perceive they are presented on television and how they react when they see a negative image of themselves. In an effort to overcome this absence of reliable information, The Tomás Rivera Policy Institute undertook a national telephone survey of Latinos and Non-Hispanic whites in the five states with the largest Latino populations. The survey had three interrelated goals:

1. to assess the extent to which Latinos have access to television technologies;

2. to evaluate Latino viewing behaviors including languages used and types of programs watched; and

3. to determine how Latinos react to their portrayals.

We found Latinos to be active consumers of both Spanish and English television and to be higher volume consumers than non-Hispanic whites. Overall, Latinos expressed mixed emotions about their portrayal on television. They expressed contentment when asked general questions about the presentation of Latino stories on English-language news programs and the presentation of Latino characters on English-language entertainment programs. However, they found particular fault with the subject matter of news programs when they covered Latinos and saw many of the characters on entertainment programs as putting Latinos in a negative light.

Spanish-language television also was the target of ambivalent feelings. Latinos reported that Spanish television was less likely than English television to present sexual content and violence and generally presented Latinos in a positive light. Yet, Latinos with children in their households reported that Spanish television did not present enough educational programming for children. These same respondents took children's programming on English-language television to task for not presenting enough positive role models for their children.

The survey demonstrated that Latinos are not simply passive viewers of the medium. Almost half of our respondents reported that when confronted with a negative stereotype, they have turned off the program. Further, approximately one in six purchased a product because an advertiser used a Latino actor in a commercial.

In sum, this first national study of Latino portrayals on television presents a rich and nuanced portrait of how Latinos see themselves on television. Based on their responses, we identify four broad recommendations to government and to the television industry about how to improve Latinos' attitudes toward the medium.

Introduction

Do Hispanics[1] see themselves on television?

Do Latinos think that they are presented positively or negatively when they do see themselves?

Which language television do Latinos watch?

Do Latinos feel that they are better served by English-language television, Spanish-language television, or both?

How do they react when they see an image on television that they find offensive?

With the rapid growth of the Latino population, questions such as these are becoming more salient. Yet, despite the community's population growth and increasing economic role in U.S. society, there is little reliable data to assess the interaction between Latinos and television –the nearly universal medium that informs us of the world around us and helps shape our opinions. In an effort to establish a baseline understanding of Hispanic use of television and Latino portrayals on television, we conducted a survey of 1,013 Latinos and 404 non-Hispanic whites (hereafter, Anglos) in the five states with the largest Latino populations (California, Texas, New York, Florida, and Illinois). The survey had three interrelated goals:

1. to assess the extent to which Latinos have access to television technologies;

2. to evaluate Latino viewing behaviors including languages used and types of programs watched; and

3. to determine how Latinos react to their portrayals.

This study is the first of its kind at a national level and offers a rich, and otherwise unavailable, public source of data to allow Latinos to talk back to television.

In this report, we analyze the results of this study. We begin with analysis of Latino access to television and their use of various television technologies. As we indicate, they are a "tuned in" population. We then examine television-viewing behaviors, including the questions of language of television watched and children's viewing behaviors. We then discuss Latino attitudes toward television. Overall, Latinos say they are moderately favorable of television generally and of specific programming options, but they also offer some pointed criticisms and concerns about the range of options that they have on television.

We also present Hispanic perceptions of comparisons between English-language and Spanish-language television,
of children's programming, and of how Latinos reacted to
positive and negative images that they have seen on television. We conclude with some policy recommendations that
emerge from the survey. For readers interested in the structure of the survey and the characteristics of the survey respondents, Appendix One describes how we conducted the
survey and compares our respondents to the Latino population as a whole in the five states where we undertook the
survey. Appendix Two presents the actual survey questionnaire and responses by Latinos and Anglos, as well as information on language of television most frequently
watched—Spanish, English, or both equally.

Televisions and television equipment in the household: A tuned-in population

The revolution in television technologies has reached Latino
communities. More than 99 percent of Hispanic households
have a working television set in their homes. The average
Latino household had approximately 2.3 televisions, with almost 10 percent having four or more (see Table One). Most
Latino households had access to cable (62 percent) and more
than five-in-six (85 percent) had video cassette recorders
(VCRs). Nearly half had televisions that allow for language
translation (SAP devices). Satellite connections, on the other
hand, were somewhat less common at only 13 percent.

Hispanic households had slightly lower rates than Anglo
households in terms of number of televisions owned, access
to cable and ownership of VCRs. Anglo households owned
2.7 televisions on average. Three-quarters of Anglo households had cable connections and almost nine in 10 had VCRs.
Latino households were slightly more likely than Anglo households to be connected to satellite television.

Most Latino households could receive Spanish-language
television stations clearly. This included households that had
access to cable and those that did not. Only 7 percent of
Hispanic respondents in the five states reported that their
households did not receive Spanish stations clearly. Interestingly, respondents in households that could receive it
clearly, nevertheless, reported in some cases that they watched

	Table 1. Equipment	
	Latinos	**Anglos**
Television Equipment		
Average number of working TV sets in house	2.3	2.7
TV sets connected to:		
Cable	62.1%	75.0%
Satellite	12.4%	10.9%
A VCR	84.7%	89.6%
TV set equipped with a language translation device (SAP)	46.0%	Not asked
Receive Spanish-language station clearly	93.0%	Not asked
Hours of television watched daily		
None	1.3%	0.7%
Less than 1 hour	3.4%	6.7%
1 to 3 hours	30.7%	48.0%
4 to 5 hours	34.1%	25.7%
More than 5 hours	30.2%	18.8%

Spanish-language television primarily or in combination with English-language television. This finding indicates that Spanish-language television continues to have a market to expand its breadth across the country and its service to meet the needs of future immigrants, the primary viewers of Spanish language television.

Latino households reported watching television extensively. Fully 30 percent of respondents reported watching more than five hours of television each day and another 34 percent watched four to five hours daily. Only 31 percent of Latinos watched one to three hours daily. Latino television viewership for many respondents included daily watching both Spanish *and* English television.

The comparable viewership rates for Anglo households were lower with 19 percent watching more than five hours each day and another 26 percent watching four to five hours daily. Nearly half (48 percent) watch between one and three hours daily. This finding – that Latinos watch more television than Anglos – is consistent with previous research.

**Latino presence on English-language television—
Not quite ready for prime time?**
A second tool for understanding Latinos and television is to examine how Latinos see themselves on television. To answer

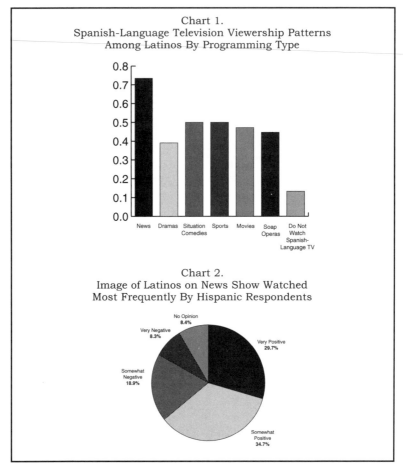

Chart 1.
Spanish-Language Television Viewership Patterns
Among Latinos By Programming Type

Chart 2.
Image of Latinos on News Show Watched
Most Frequently By Hispanic Respondents

this question, we asked respondents who said they watched English-language television some or all of the time whether the English-language programs that they watch showed Hispanics.

Our respondents indicated that they saw few Latinos on the English-language news and entertainment programming they watched. Less that 40 percent, for example, reported that there was a Hispanic anchor or newscaster on the English-language news program they watched *most* frequently. Similarly, on English-language entertainment programs they watched, just 7 percent reported that there were always Latino characters and nearly 42 percent said that there were never Latino characters on these programs. Finally, the majority said that advertising on English-language television also neglected

Latino characters; approximately 57 percent reported that commercials rarely or never presented Latino characters.

As we will note later, survey respondents reported that Latinos were often presented negatively on television, particularly on English-language television. Nevertheless, the frequent absence of Latinos and Latino characters on English-language television was a consistent message of survey respondents. This finding reinforces several earlier studies that employed content-analysis to evaluate English-language television networks' inclusion of Latinos.

Although the absence of Latinos and Latino characters on English-language television was a consistent finding, there was some variation across the states under study. Half of Latinos in Texas and California reported that their most watched news program had a Latino anchor or newscaster. In contrast, just one in five New Yorkers had a similar response. California and Texas respondents were also slightly more likely to report that Latino characters appeared in commercials they saw on English-language television.

Interestingly, Anglo respondents reported a slightly *greater* presence of Latinos, at least on entertainment programming, perhaps reflecting a lower awareness of Latinos on television. While few Anglos reported that there were always Latino characters on entertainment programming they watched, more than 60 percent reported that this was sometimes the case (compared to just 42 percent of Hispanics who "sometimes" observed Latinos in entertainment programming).

In terms of commercials and news programming on the other hand, Anglos were less likely to see Latinos than were Latinos themselves. Slightly less than one-third of Anglos reported that their most watched news show had a Latino anchor or newscaster, a rate approximately eight percent lower than for Latinos. We present these comparisons with some caution since we assume that Anglos are generally less aware of Latinos on television than are Hispanics[2].

In sum, Latinos have access to television technologies comparable to Anglos in the states where they reside. Most have access to clear transmissions of Spanish-language programming and, as we indicated earlier, watch both English- and Spanish-language programming. For those who did watch English-language news, entertainment, and commercial programming, few reported seeing Latinos on any of these programs, an opinion largely shared by Anglos in these five states.

Television viewing behaviors

As we have indicated, Latinos reported that they watched quite a bit of television. This statement only tells part of the story. The vast majority (approximately 75 percent) watched television in both Spanish *and* English.

In the discussion that follows, we will analyze the types of programs watched on Spanish and English television. We will also distinguish the behaviors of Latinos based on the *primary* language of their television viewing – those who watch television primarily or exclusively in Spanish (26 percent), those who reported that they watch both equally (50 percent), and those who watch television primarily or exclusively in English (24 percent). Only 13 percent reported that they watched television *exclusively* in English and 11 percent watched *exclusively* in Spanish.

Language of Television Programming

The language in which the respondent watched television reflects where they were born. The majority of Latinos born in the United States watched English-language television and a large minority watched both Spanish and English equally (see Table Two). Just 11 percent of U.S.-born Latinos watched Spanish television primarily or exclusively (all of whom were born in Puerto Rico). Among immigrant Latinos, the pattern of television viewership was somewhat reversed. More than half of foreign-born Latinos watched programming in both Spanish and English in roughly equal amounts. Only 29 percent, however, relied on Spanish exclusively or primarily and 14 percent watched English television primarily or exclusively. These English-language viewing immigrants tended to have immigrated to the United States at a young age or were highly educated. Overall, then, immigrants were much more likely to rely on English programming than the U.S.-born were on Spanish programming.

These findings indicate that the primary demand for Spanish programming comes from immigrants, who constitute approximately 40 percent of the Latino population nationally. While some U.S.-born Latinos watch both Spanish and English television, the majority were English-dominant in their viewership patterns. Thus, if these television language use patterns were to continue and if immigration were to slow, the demand for Spanish-language television could decline over

Table 2. Nativity and Language of Television Viewership		
	U.S. born %	Foreign born %
Exclusively English	28.4	7.1
Primarily English	24.6	7.1
Both languages equally	35.6	55.9
Primarily Spanish	4.2	16.2
Exclusively Spanish	6.9	12.9
(n)	288	718

time. At present, however, the Spanish-language television audience increases each year with new immigrants to the United States.

The use of Spanish- and English- language programming varied by programming type. News was the programming most likely to be watched in both languages. Almost 74 percent of Latinos watched news on Spanish-language television. This means that 85 percent of Latinos who watch anything on Spanish-language television watch the news, since 13 percent of Latinos watched no Spanish-language programming.

Viewership of Spanish-language news programs did not preclude also watching English-language news programming. Only 26 percent of respondents watched the news exclusively in Spanish. A roughly equal number watched the news primarily or exclusively in English and 40 percent watched news programs in Spanish and English equally. Only 4 percent of respondents reported that they did not watch any news programs at all.

Viewership rates for other programs on Spanish-language television were lower. Approximately 39 percent of Latinos watched dramas on Spanish television, 45 percent watched soap operas, 47 percent watched movies, and 50 percent watched situation comedies or sports. Thus, news was the most watched program on Spanish television by a large margin. Depending on the type of Spanish-television programming, gender differences appeared. Hispanic women were more likely to watch soap operas and dramas while Hispanic men were more likely to watch situation comedies and sports in Spanish.

Entertainment programs also reached audiences in English, though in somewhat smaller numbers than did the news. Approximately 57 percent of Latino respondents reported that they watched entertainment programs in English.

Interestingly, a much smaller share watched entertainment and drama programs in both Spanish *and* English. Just 20 percent of Latinos tapped both Spanish and English entertainment programming, and just under 20 percent did not watch these programs at all in either language.

In addition to the bilingual nature of Latino viewership behaviors, particularly for news programming, a second behavioral pattern appeared. Television watching was a family affair (a pattern that also appeared in Anglo households). More than 60 percent of Latinos watched television with family members; slightly more than one-third of respondents commonly watched television alone. Those respondents who watched equal amounts of Spanish and English television were the most likely to watch television with family members. This may reflect the multilingual nature of many Latino households. The bilingual viewer is most likely to have the linguistic skills to watch television with all members of the household.

Adults in Latino households were more likely than Ango adults to report that children in their households watched television with adults. More than 40 percent of the children in Latino households watched television with adult family members compared to 27 percent in Anglo households. Again, adults who reported that they watched television in English and Spanish in roughly equal amounts were most likely to report that children in the household watched television with adults.

The language of children's television in Latino households
Children in Latino households watched English television much more than did the adults. More than 70 percent of respondents reported that the children in their household watched television more in English than in Spanish. Just 5 percent watched more Spanish than English and approximately 27 percent watched both equally. While the television language use patterns of the respondent did seem to influence the reported viewership language of children, it is important to note that even in households where the respondent watched Spanish-language television primarily or exclusively, almost 60percent of the children watched more English than Spanish television. Thus, children in Spanish-dominant Latino households are rapidly joining the pool of English-language television viewers. As we note below, this use of English-language television among children in Hispanic households may reflect the poor choices available to them on Spanish-television.

There is virtually no evidence from the survey that English-dominant and bilingual households use Spanish-language television to encourage bilingualism among household children. In households where the respondent watched primarily or exclusively English television, just 6 percent of household children watched more Spanish television or Spanish and English equally. In households with respondents who watched English and Spanish television equally, only 5 percent of the children watched more Spanish television and 28 percent watched English and Spanish equally. If these patterns continue as today's children age, they indicate that Spanish-language television may be less important to them than to their parents.

How do Latinos feel about what they see on TV?

Latinos react in two somewhat contradictory manners to what they see on television. In response to general questions about the overall images of Latinos on television and to more specific questions about different types of programs on English- and Spanish-language television, they offered mildly favorable evaluations. When probed on more specific questions –such as the presence of Latino characters, the roles that Hispanics play on television, the content of stories about Latinos on the news, and the presence of positive stereotypes for Hispanic children on television – they offered a more negative portrait. While these opinions may seem contradictory, they reflect an audience that is an active, if not wholly content, consumer of what television has to offer. They are, then, both satisfied and dissatisfied and seek a more complete and nuanced picture of Latinos on television. As we will indicate, they react to negative images and will turn off programs that contain negative stereotypes.

Evaluating the medium
We sought both a general evaluation of television from our respondents and more specific evaluations of news and entertainment programming. While we found that overall Latinos were more satisfied than dissatisfied with what they see on television, we also found variations based on the language of programming most watched. Viewers of Spanish television were generally more satisfied than viewers of English television. Those who view both Spanish and English television equally fell in between these extremes.

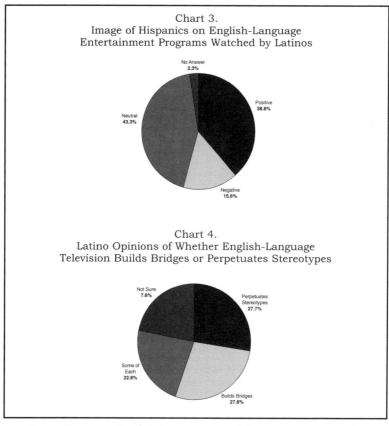

Chart 3.
Image of Hispanics on English-Language
Entertainment Programs Watched by Latinos

No Answer
2.3%

Positive
38.8%

Neutral
43.3%

Negative
15.6%

Chart 4.
Latino Opinions of Whether English-Language
Television Builds Bridges or Perpetuates Stereotypes

Not Sure
7.6%

Perpetuates
Stereotypes
27.7%

Some of
Each
22.8%

Builds Bridges
27.6%

Overall, more than 60 percent of Hispanics reported that the image presented of Latinos on the English-language news show that they watch most frequently was very positive or somewhat positive. Approximately 30 percent reported that the image of Latinos was very positive and 35 percent reported that it was somewhat positive. At the other extreme, only 8 percent said that Latinos were presented in a very negative manner. Hispanics who watched exclusively English-language television were slightly more negative about English-language news programs, with just 55 percent saying that the presentation of Latinos on the most watched news show was either very positive or somewhat positive.

Of those Anglo respondents with an opinion, more than 70 percent reported that the news presented Latinos in a very positive or somewhat positive light. We take this finding with some caution since almost one-third of Anglos did not venture an opinion.

In terms of entertainment programming on English-language television, approximately 40 percent of Latino respondents reported that Latinos were presented in a positive light. Surprisingly, just 16 percent reported that English-language entertainment programming presented Latinos negatively and 45 percent saw the presentation as neutral.

Again, viewers of Spanish-language television were somewhat more positive overall than viewers of English-language television. More than 46 percent of those who primarily viewed Spanish television saw the portrayal of Latinos as positive on English-language entertainment programs.

Anglos, again, saw the portrayal of Latinos to be positive or benign. Slightly less than 43 percent said that Latinos were presented positively and 47 percent said they were presented in neutral terms.

These specific findings concerning news and entertainment programming are reinforced by a question that sought to obtain an overall evaluation of the presentation of Latinos on television (here not limited to English-language television). To assess this question, we used a "feeling thermometer," a survey strategy that asks respondents to rate the overall presentation of Latinos on all aspects of television using the notion of a thermometer. Respondents were instructed to rate television from 1 to 100, with 1 being cold and 100 being hot. Overall, Latinos offered television a modestly positive evaluation—a 61 on the scale of 100. Unexpectedly, this ranking was exactly the same as the ranking offered by Anglos (though a higher percentage of Anglos did not offer an answer to this question).

Again, there was some variation by the language of television programs watched with the viewers of Spanish television generally more positive (a score of 68) and the viewers of English-language television generally more negative (a score of 56). Viewers of both Spanish and English television fell in the middle (a score of 61).

The overall satisfaction with the presentation of Latinos on television increased with the volume of television consumed. Latinos who viewed less than one hour per day ranked television's presentation of Latinos at just 56, those who viewed 1 to 3 hours daily gave television a 60. This increased to 61 among the viewers of 4 to 5 hours daily and 65 among the those who watched television more than 5 hours a day.

We also asked respondents to evaluate the overall quality of Spanish-language television. We asked this question only of respondents who reported that they watched Spanish-language television. Here, we did not use the feeling thermometer device, but instead asked whether they believed that Spanish-language television presented a positive, negative, or neutral image of Latinos. Approximately 45 percent of respondents reported that it presented a positive image and only 15 percent perceived a negative image. Respondents who routinely watch Spanish television were even more likely to place Spanish television in a positive light, with 56 percent viewing it positively and just 10 percent saying that it presents Latinos in a negative light.

In sum, Latinos reported an overall satisfaction with the way in which Spanish- and English-language television portrays Latinos. These levels of satisfaction varied somewhat by the specific type and language of programming, but showed that Latinos were content with the overall presentation of Latinos on programming available through television. As we indicate in subsequent sections, this contentment is not uncritical. Instead, Latinos provided pointed criticisms of aspects of television, but these overall evaluations are important because they demonstrate that despite some criticisms, Latinos like how they see themselves on television.

Criticisms and concerns
Despite these favorable overall evaluations, Latinos criticized the programs they watched. These criticisms fit into three broad categories. First, as we have already discussed, they reported the absence of Latinos on television. Second, when they did see Hispanics on television, whether as a character on a drama or commercial or in news coverage about the Latino community, our respondents observed that Hispanics were more often presented negatively than positively (particularly in news programming). Finally, respondents were concerned that English-language television perpetuates stereotypes about the Latino community. Interestingly, respondents reported that they take action to oppose these stereotypes.

The first concern about television content that appears in survey responses was the absence of Latinos on television. We have already discussed this in some depth, but it bears repeating that for the majority of Latinos, there was no Latino

Table 3.
Topics of Coverage of Stories Concerning
Latino Men and Women on English-language News Programs

| | **Latinos** | | **Anglos** |
| | Stories Concerning Latino Men | Stories Concerning Latina Women | Stories Concerning Latinos |
	%	%	%
Crime	34.1	13.3	17.7
Immigration/illegal immigration	24.8	16.4	15.2
Drugs	6.3	2.8	2.5
Politics and elections/ elected officials	5.0	2.8	5.0
Sports	3.9	1.9	3.9
Education	3.1	7.4	6.9
Victims of crime	3.1	17.2	1.7
Other	7.4	12.8	7.8
Never covers Latinos	2.6	3.6	1.9
Don't know	9.8	21.8	37.4

Table 4.
Images of Latino Men and Women on
English-language Entertainment Programs
(Among Respondents Who Could Identify an Image)

| | Images of Latino Men | Images of Latina Women |
	%	%
Positive/good image	14.7	15.0
Criminal/crook	12.0	-
Detective/police	10.9	2.4
Negative image	10.3	5.4
Comedian/funny	8.2	3.0
Gang member	6.0	-
Latin lover/womanizer	6.0	-
Ignorant/dumb/uneducated	5.4	4.2
Sports star/athlete	4.9	-
Unemployed/poor person	3.3	-
Maid/servant	-	15.0
Prostitute/wild woman	-	9.0
Housewife	-	7.2
Victim	-	7.2
Professional	-	3.6
Pregnant woman	-	2.4
Sophisticated	-	2.4
Other	18.3	23.4

anchor or newscaster on the English-language news program most frequently watched. Also, nearly 42 percent said that there were never Latino characters on the English-language entertainment programs they watched. Furthermore, approximately 57 percent reported that commercials rarely or never presented Latino characters. So, while Latinos are active consumers of television, their attachment is largely unreciprocated by the medium.

So, while we could not fully measure Latinos' perceptions of how this absence impacted their attitudes toward television, we did probe their perceptions of the benefits of having a Latino anchor or newscaster. More than 67 percent reported that having a Hispanic anchor or newscaster improved the quality of coverage of the Latino community.

A second concern is even more damning in light of the first. Our respondents reported that Latinos were most often presented in a negative light when Latinos appeared on English-language entertainment programming, or when the Hispanic community was covered by English-language news[3]. When asked to identify the most frequent topic of news stories that included Latino men, crime and immigration/"illegal" immigration topped the list (see Table Three). These two themes alone accounted for more than half the stories concerning Latino men. When Latinas were the focus of the story, the most common theme was "victims of crime," followed by immigration/"illegal" immigration and crime.

Story themes that are more likely to present Latinos and the Latino community in a positive light appear in much smaller numbers. Politics and elected officials, for example, represented just 6 percent of stories concerning Latino men and 3 percent of stories concerning Hispanic women. Education and sports stories, that potentially present Hispanics very positively, were also the subject of few stories.

Anglos were much less likely to be able to identify topics of news coverage of Latinos. Fully 37 percent could not identify such a topic. Of those Anglos who did identify Latino-related news topics, the most frequently identified topics were crime and immigration/illegal aliens.

Entertainment programming on English-language television received a mixed evaluation, with reports of both positive and negative images from Latino respondents (see Table Four). There were also quite different perceptions of how Latino men and women are portrayed. The most common image was

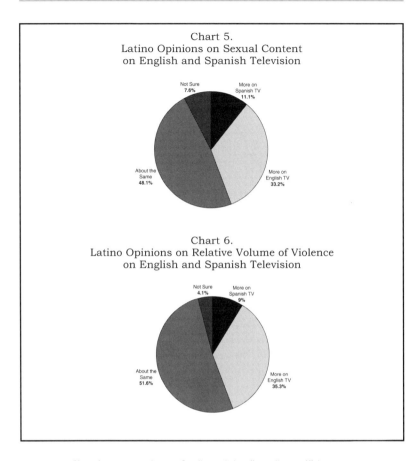

Chart 5.
Latino Opinions on Sexual Content
on English and Spanish Television

Not Sure 7.6%
More on Spanish TV 11.1%
About the Same 48.1%
More on English TV 33.2%

Chart 6.
Latino Opinions on Relative Volume of Violence
on English and Spanish Television

Not Sure 4.1%
More on Spanish TV 9%
About the Same 51.6%
More on English TV 35.3%

a generalized perception of a "positive" or "good" image. Among images of Hispanic women, this reported "positive image" was tied with the image of a maid or servant. The third most common image of Hispanic women was prostitutes. The third most common images for Hispanic men were detectives or police. While these images are conflicting, they show that when Hispanics appeared on English-language entertainment programming, the images tended to be more a combination of positive and negative images than on the news. Overall, however, many negative images on television reflect little of the reality of roles that Latinos occupy in U.S. society.

Latinos were of mixed opinions on whether English-language television perpetuated stereotypes of Latinos or built bridges between Latinos and other groups in U.S. society. Almost equal numbers of respondents (approximately 28 percent) took each of these positions. A slightly smaller number said that elements of each of these positions were accurate and approximately 22 percent were not sure. Perhaps unexpectedly, regular viewers of English-language television took the most negative view. More than 36 percent of Latino respondents said that English television perpetuates negative stereotypes.

Anglo respondents took a somewhat different view. A plurality (approximately 41 percent) reported that television builds bridges between groups in society. Just one in five Anglos reported that television perpetuated stereotypes.

Latinos, then, reported an overall contentment with television, with specific types of programming on English-language programming, and with the image that Spanish-language television projects of Hispanics, but they also offered some pointed criticisms. Specifically, they noted the absence of Latinos, and saw a potential cost in the quality of coverage of Latinos on the news from this absence. They also reported that many of the images of Latinos presented in news and entertainment programming were negative, particularly on news programming, and they perceived that English-language television was more likely to perpetuate stereotypes than to build bridges. Overall, viewers of English language television were more likely to be critical of the medium than were viewers of Spanish-language television.

Spanish and English television: Comparisons of content
Since such a large share of our Latino respondents are active consumers of television in both Spanish *and* English (approximately 75 percent of respondents), we designed the survey to ask respondents to compare the two media on two controversies surrounding broadcast television, specifically sex and violence. Interestingly, most Latinos who had an opinion on both Spanish and English programming reported that the level of sexual content and the amount of violence was about the same on both. In both cases, these opinions were held by narrow majorities. Approximately one-third of respondents to each question reported that there was more sex and more violence on English-language television. These general patterns were consistent regardless of the language of television most watched by the respondent.

However, in the presentation of violence on English-language television, survey respondents identified a particular problem. The majority reported that Latinos were more likely

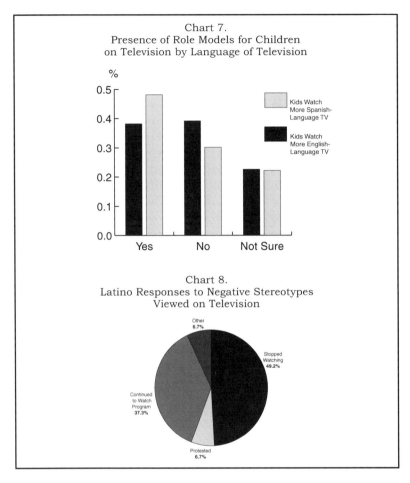

Chart 7.
Presence of Role Models for Children
on Television by Language of Television

%

- Kids Watch More Spanish-Language TV
- Kids Watch More English-Language TV

Yes   No   Not Sure

Chart 8.
Latino Responses to Negative Stereotypes
Viewed on Television

Other
6.7%

Stopped
Watching
49.2%

Continued
to Watch
Program
37.3%

Protested
6.7%

to be presented as violent on English-language television than on Spanish-language television. These beliefs were most strongly held by regular viewers of Spanish-language television.

While not definitive due to the relatively small number of questions asking respondents to compare English- and Spanish-language television, it is clear that Latinos have greater concerns about the content of English-language television than Spanish-language television, especially when it comes to controversial issues such as sex and violence. Viewers of both languages represent three in four Latinos, so despite their reported likelihood to watch English television, they are relatively less happy with what they see.

Children's programming

Latinos expressed concerns about the content of children's programming. As we will indicate, Latinos felt there was too little educational programming on Spanish-language television. At the same time, when asked about positive role models for children, respondendents reported that these were absent from English-language television.

More than two-thirds of respondents who had an opinion about Spanish-language children's television reported that they strongly agreed with the statement that there were not enough educational programs for children on Spanish television. Another 20 percent somewhat agreed with this position. These positions were held even more strongly by respondents who watched Spanish television primarily or exclusively or who watched both Spanish and English equally, who presumably were best positioned to evaluate Spanish-language children's television.

A second concern about the content of children's television was the absence of role models for kids on television. Slightly more than one-third reported that there were positive role models and a roughly equal number said that there were not. This even distribution masks a larger phenomenon. Adults who reported that their children watched Spanish television were more likely to report positive images on children's television than were those whose children watched English-language television. More than 48 percent of respondents who reported that the children in the household watched Spanish television also reported that there were positive role models for children on television.

Since the majority of children in Latino households watched English-language television, the higher availability of positive role models on Spanish-language television is problematic. Despite this seeming endorsement of Spanish-language television children's programming, at least relative to English-language programming, this finding must be tempered by the strong concern that respondents expressed about the absence of children's educational programs on Spanish-language television.

Anglos were much more likely to report that there were positive role models for children. More than 60 percent felt that positive children's role models were available for their children. This finding may reflect, in part, the fact that there is a greater diversity of children's programming on English-language television and that adults in Anglo households were less likely to watch television with the household's children.

Reacting to television

Finally, we sought to find out how Latinos reacted to what they saw on television. We sought to test how they reacted to positive and negative presentations. As we will indicate, many Latinos reported that they turned off programs with negative stereotypes.

Approximately one-third of Latino respondents reported that they had seen a program that negatively stereotyped Latinos. English-language television viewers were almost twice as likely as viewers of Spanish-television to report having seen these stereotypes. More than half of the respondents who reported having seen a stereotype on a television program reported that this was on English-language programming and another third reported that they had seen stereotypes on both English and Spanish programming. A relatively small number (approximately 10 percent) reported that they had seen a negative stereotype about Latinos on Spanish-language television.

What have Latinos done when faced with these negative stereotypes? A near majority simply turned off the program. This reaction was somewhat more common among viewers of Spanish-language television. Almost 60 percent of these viewers turned off the offending program. A somewhat smaller number, only 7 percent of Latino respondents, said they protested the offensive image in some manner.

Overall, Anglos were less likely to see stereotypes and much less likely to react to the stereotype. Only 25 percent reported that they had seen a negative stereotype of Latinos. Of those that had, just 22 percent turned off the program and 2 percent protested. Clearly, then, Latinos are the ones who see these problems and must communicate them to television programmers.

We also sought to evaluate how Latinos reacted when they saw a more positive image. Here we tapped their behaviors when an advertiser used a Latino actor in a commercial. The presence of a Hispanic actor had little effect on Latino buying behavior. Yet, 17 percent reported that they had purchased a product simply because a Latino pitched the product. Since there are few Latinos in commercials, this low rate of having acted on seeing a Hispanic actor in a commercial could, in fact, reflect considerable influence. This pattern was consistent regardless of the language of television viewed.

We also probed Latino attitudes on the current use of a Latino images in advertising – the Taco Bell commercials featuring a Chihuahua that alternatively speaks English and Spanish and evokes Latino and Latin American imagery. Despite criticisms from some that the commercial is offensive, slightly more than two-thirds of Hispanic respondents and three-quarters of Anglo respondents reported that these commercials were funny. From an advertiser's perspective, these commercials got much popular attention, though more with Anglos than Latinos. Approximately 70 percent of Latinos reported familiarity with the commercial as did 86 percent of Anglos.

In sum, these findings indicate that when confronted with a negative stereotype, nearly half of Latinos turned off the program. A smaller, though not insignificant number, protested. Finally, Latinos, at least in the case of the current Taco Bell commercial, do not automatically take offense at the use of Latino imagery and use of Spanish that is offensive to some community leaders to sell a product to the national market.

Conclusions and Policy Recommendations

Thus survey of Latino television use and portrayals of Latinos on television answers some questions about Latino television viewing and attitudes toward television that could not previously be answered. It reveals that Latino adults are actively engaged with television in both Spanish and English at levels higher than Anglos. Respondents also reported that for Latino children, English viewing is more common. New television technologies are widely used in Latino communities. Overall, Latinos reported that they were content with television and with news and entertainment programs on English television. Despite this contentment, they identified some specific concerns. High among these was the dearth of Latinos on television and the roles played by or the events reported about Latinos when they do appear. Latinos perceived that the presence of Hispanic news anchors raised the likelihood that the Latino community would be presented in a positive light on news programs.

Both Spanish and English television are taken to task. Spanish-language television is perceived not to have sufficient children's programming, although to be more likely than

English television to present positive role models in children's programming. English television, on the other hand, is perceived to have too much sex and violence, relative to Spanish television. It is also perceived to present too many negative stereotypes of Latinos, and to divide groups in the society rather than to build bridges. Latinos also reported that they acted when they saw stereotypes that they did not like.

Overall, viewers of Spanish-language television were more satisfied with what they saw on television than were viewers of both Spanish and English or respondents who primarily viewed English-language broadcasts. While this may indicate that Spanish-language television is more in tune with the needs and interests of the Latino community, it may also reflect characteristics of those who primarily watch Spanish-language television – immigrants to the United States. Other studies indicate that immigrants are less likely to perceive discrimination and, hence, may be less critical of what they view. In the end, watching television is voluntary. Those who watch the most television, regardless of what language the view, are the most satisfied with what it presents.

Policy recommendations

The results of the survey lead the Tomás Rivera Policy Institute to issue four policy recommendations to address concerns raised by Latino respondents to the survey.

First, the concern about the availability of children's programming on Spanish-language television indicates that policy discussions about the need for educational programming on all broadcast stations should include Spanish-language stations in the discussion. Parents are clearly dissatisfied with what is available; children are voting with their channel selectors by watching more English-language programs. Thus, licensing standards requiring educational programming on Spanish-language television must be enforced and standards must be raised.

A second and related concern is the overwhelming number of Hispanic children who watch English-language television. Programming that recognizes the large numbers of Hispanic children should take their linguistic and educational needs into account.

Third, news programming on English-language stations must take into consideration the concerns expressed by Latinos about both their absence from the news and the roles in which they appear when news on Latinos is presented. Overwhelmingly, Latinos watch the news. Yet, they are more dissatisfied by the images they see here than they are with images in entertainment programming. Here again, license renewals offer the opportunity for community leaders to condemn stations that fail to cover Latinos or that cover them, but present them in a negative light.

Finally, the dearth of Latinos on television and their portrayals when they do appear offers a challenge to broadcasters. This survey demonstrates definitively that many Latinos are now consumers of English-language broadcasting and many more soon will be. Unless English-language broadcasters want to alienate one of their fastest growing audiences, they must be more attentive to the concerns of their Hispanic audience. Our survey indicates that Latinos wanted to talk back to television. They offered praise as well as criticism. Behaviorally, instead of protesting their concerns to the television industry, they simply surfed away by changing channels. Television executives and corporate sponsors should bear this in mind as they make programming decisions that exclude Latinos or present them in a disproportionately negative light.

Notes

The author would like to acknowledge the assistance of the many individuals who made this research project and this report possible. I would like to thank Harry P Pachon and Rodolfo O. de la Garza, the Tomás Rivera Policy Institute's President and Vice President for Research respectively, for their invaluable assistance in identifying themes for inquiry and recommending strategies that ensured the methodological rigor and objectivity of the research. I would also like to thank Sarah Banet-Weiser and Federico Subervi-Vélez for their thoughtful observations on existing scholarly research, themes for our survey, and key findings. That they offered this assistance on a tight timeline makes my appreciation even greater. I would also like to thank the staff and summer fellows of the TRPI for their wide range of suggestions for possible survey questions.

Finally, this project and, more importantly, this report would not have been possible without four TRPI staff members who assisted me throughout the project. Karen Escalante-Dalton, TRPI

Vice President of Operations, assisted at every stage of the project, provided a sounding board for ideas and concerns, and ensured that the report would be produced. Miguel Baraona translated the survey questionnaire into Spanish. Joy Hofer edited the final draft. Rick Strycker designed the report.

This study was made possible through the generous support of Anheuser-Busch Companies, Inc., HBO, and Time Warner.

1. We use the terms Latino and Hispanic interchangeably to refer to individuals who trace their origin or ancestry to the Spanish-speaking parts of Latin America or the Caribbean.

2. In order to ensure that our Anglo respondents knew what we meant by the terms Latino and Hispanic, we offered a definition the first time that we used the term.

3. We asked these questions concerning the English-language television presentation of news stories about Latinos and the Latino community and Latinos in entertainment television only of respondents who reported that they watched English-language news and entertainment programming and, in the case of entertainment programming of those who reported that these shows always or sometimes presented Latino characters. As a result, the overall sample size is lower for these questions—646 Latino respondents for question about news topics and 363 Latinos for the question about images of Latinos on English-language entertainment programming.

Appendix One

The sample and respondent characteristics

The survey consisted of 1,013 Latino adults in the five states with the largest Latino populations (California, Florida, Illinois, New York, and Texas) and was conducted over an eleven-day period in August 1998. We selected telephone numbers randomly from a list of households with Spanish-surnamed members and listed telephone numbers. In each case, we verified that the respondent was Latino, a regular member of the household, and over 18 years of age. Our initial sampling goal was 200 respondents from each state. Due to the fact that multiple surveys were conducted at the same time, we slightly exceeded this goal in several states.

All respondents had the option of conducting the survey in Spanish or in English and all survey staff were fully bilingual. The survey instrument was translated from English to Spanish by natives of several Latin American nations in order to assure that the Spanish was appropriate for a respondent pool from all parts of Latin America and the Caribbean. Nearly 85 percent of respondents completed the survey in Spanish. The average survey took approximately 15 minutes to complete.

In order to be able to offer context and comparison for this survey of Latino television behaviors and perceptions of Latino portrayals on television, we also conducted a more narrow survey of non-Hispanic whites in the same states. This survey of Anglos included fewer respondents (404) and a shortened questionnaire that focused more on perceptions of the portrayal of Latinos on television. The average Anglo survey took approximately nine minutes to complete. Our sampling goal for the survey of Anglos was 80 respondents in each state, which we again exceeded slightly in several states.

While we have a sufficient number of respondents to compare Latinos across the five states studied or to compare Latinos with specific behaviors, the size of our Anglo sample does not allow for subgroup analysis. Among the subgroups that we analyze are Latinos who watch programming in Spanish, English, or a combination of the two, Latinos from different states, and Latinos who watch quite a bit of television on a daily basis versus those who watch smaller amounts.

Appendix Table 1. Respondent Profile		
	Latinos	Anglos
Average age	40	46
Average years of education	10.5	14.1
% with high school degree	58.0%	92.1%
Children under 18 in house	57.0%	36.1%
Gender		
Men	47.0%	47.5%
Women	53.0%	52.5%
Modal Household Income Range	$20,001- $30,000	$40,001- $50,000

Both Anglo and Latino respondents were drawn from throughout these five states. Because of residential concentration patterns, Latinos were more likely than the Anglo respondents to reside in urban or suburban areas.

Respondent characteristics
It is not possible to present a simple characterization of the average Latino or Anglo survey respondent. Respondents to the Latino survey ranged in age from 18 to 89, with an average age of 40. Although 58 percent had earned high school degrees, the average number of years of education among Latinos was 10.5. Slightly more than 70 percent of Latinos were born abroad. The median household income was between $20,001 and $30,000, although we should note that one-quarter of respondents did not disclose their household incomes (which is customary on telephone surveys such as this one). A slight majority of Latino respondents were of Mexican origin or ancestry, but the remaining 46 percent came from all parts of the Spanish-speaking Latin America and the Caribbean. Twelve percent were Central American, 11 percent were Cuban, 10 percent were Puerto Rican, 8 percent were South American, and 5 percent were Dominican. Almost six in 10 Latino households had children under 18 in the household.

Anglo respondents were generally older, more educated, and had higher household incomes than did Latinos in the survey. They were also less likely to have children in the household. Both the Latino and Anglo samples were roughly evenly divided between men and women. Appendix Table One summarizes some key demographic characteristics of Latino and Anglo respondents to the survey.

Appendix Table 2.
Demographic Characteristics of the Latino Sample

Nativity	
U.S. born	28.7%
Born abroad	71.3%
Average years of U.S. residence	
among foreign born	16.1
Percentage of life spent in	
United States (among foreign born)	
25 percent or less	29.2%
26 percent - 50 percent	43.1%
50 percent or more	27.7%
Ancestry or Origin	
Mexico	53.6%
Puerto Rico	10.2%
Cuba	10.9%
Dominican Republic	5.4%
Central America	12.0%
South America	7.9%
Self-reported language abilities	
Spanish dominant	48.6%
Bilingual	47.1%
English dominant	4.1%
Households with both U.S.-born	
and foreign-born adults	29.0%

We should note several differences between the Latino survey respondents and Latino population nationally. We believe that these differences broadly reflect the Latino populations of the five states under study and the sampling methodology used (a telephone survey, using a sample derived from households with Latino-surnamed residents and listed telephone numbers). The most important difference is that our respondents are more likely than the population as a whole to be foreign-born. These five states have the highest proportion of foreign-born Latinos, so this finding is not unexpected. The foreign-born share of our sample does, nevertheless, exceed levels for these states as a whole. A sampling frame derived from households with Spanish-surnamed members will draw more foreign-born respondents than other methods because U.S.-born households may be more likely to have unlisted numbers or be Latinos without Spanish surnames. Our sample is also slightly less educated than the Latino population as a whole. With these caveats in mind, we believe that the sample broadly captures the Latino communities of these five states. The higher-than-expected share of foreign-born Latinos should, however, be kept in mind when we discuss the language of television watched and frequency of viewing different types of programming on Spanish-language television.

Since such a large share of our sample is foreign born, it is important to note several characteristics of this population. First, many of these immigrants are long-term residents of the United States. On average, they have resided here for 16 years. Most have spent between one-quarter and half their lives in the United States. Finally, the dichotomy between immigrant and U.S.-born is somewhat false. Almost 30 percent of the households have both U.S.-born and immigrant adults.

Appendix Two

Survey of Television Technologies, Evaluation of the Content of Television Programming, and the Portrayal of Latinos on Television

| | Latinos % | Anglos % | Latinos who Watch | | |
			Spanish %	Both %	English %
A. Let me begin by asking whether you would prefer to speak in Spanish or English?					
Spanish	84.4	NA	97.5	90.5	60.4
English	15.6	NA	2.5	9.5	39.6
Screener 1] Are you Latino or of Hispanic origin?					
Yes	100%				
Screener 2] Are you 18 years of age or older and live as a permanent member of the household?					
Yes	100%				
[Repeat introduction if necessary]					
Screener 3] I would like to ask you a few questions so that we will be able to compare your answers to those of other people like you. Can you please tell me your age?					
Average	39.8	46.2	45.4	37.6	38.4
Screener 4] How many years of schooling have you completed?					
Average	10.5	14.2	8.3	10.6	12.2
Screener 5] What is the highest degree that you have received? [Asked of respondents 12 or more years of education]					
High school	66.3	46.9	69.9	70.1	58.9
Associate	10.6	16.7	10.8	8.1	14.4
BA/BS	9.8	22.3	6.5	9.7	11.4
Advanced degree	10.6	12.7	8.6	9.1	13.9
No degree	2.7	1.3	4.3	2.9	1.5
Screener 6] Can you tell me where you were born?					
United States	22.1	NA	9.5	13.7	50.0
Mexico	37.9	NA	49.4	45.3	12.7
Puerto Rico	6.6	NA	3.7	6.7	8.8
Cuba	9.9	NA	16.2	8.7	6.5
Dominican Republic	5.1	NA	4.1	5.7	4.6
El Salvador	3.6	NA	4.6	4.4	1.2
Other Central America	7.4	NA	7.5	7.3	7.3
South America	6.7	NA	4.6	7.5	6.9
No Answer	0.9	NA	0.4	0.6	1.9

	Latinos %	Anglos %	Latinos who Watch		
			Spanish %	Both %	English %

Screener 7] How many years have you lived in the United States? [Asked of people born abroad]

Average	16.2	NA	16.2	15.1	19.9

Screener 8] Would you say that you understand spoken [language other than interview language]?

Very well	20.4	NA	5.0	18.0	39.4
Well	26.6	NA	14.6	29.5	32.0
Not very well	34.7	NA	36.7	40.4	21.6
Not at all	18.3	NA	43.8	12.1	6.9

Screener 9] Are there children under the age of 18 who are regular residents of your household?

Yes	57.0	36.1	46.9	62.0	56.5
No	43.0	63.9	53.1	38.0	43.5

[Ask if born in the United States from Screener 6]
Screener 10] Are there adults who live as a permanent member of your household, that were born outside of the United States?

Yes	31.5	NA	26.1	42.0	26.9
No	68.5	NA	73.9	58.0	73.1

[Ask if born outside [including Puerto Rico] the United States from Screener 6]
Screener 11] Are there adults who live as a permanent member of your household, that were born in the United States?

Yes	28.2	NA	23.4	28.0	36.2
No	71.8	NA	76.6	72.0	63.8

Screener 12] Gender

Male	47.0	47.5	35.3	49.3	53.5
Female	53.0	52.5	64.7	50.7	46.5

1. How many working TV sets do you have in your home?

0	0.8	0.0	0.8	0.8	0.8
1	27.7	23.0	39.8	24.8	22.3
2	38.3	34.2	35.3	42.1	33.8
3	23.5	26.5	17.4	23.0	30.0
4 or more	9.7	16.3	6.6	9.3	13.1

2. Are any of your televisions connected to [Skip if 0 tv sets owned]:
a) Cable

Yes	62.4	75.0	54.4	61.1	72.1
No	37.6	25.0	45.6	38.9	27.9

b) Satellite

Yes	12.6	11.0	13.9	13.4	10.1
No	87.4	89.0	86.1	86.6	89.9

	Latinos %	Anglos %	Latinos who Watch		
			Spanish %	Both %	English %
c) A video-cassette recorder					
Yes	84.9	89.6	77.0	85.8	90.3
No	15.1	10.4	23.0	14.2	9.7
3. Are any of your televisions equipped with a language translation device [SAP]?					
Yes	46.0	NA	31.4	48.3	55.0
No	51.3	NA	63.2	49.7	43.4
Not sure	2.7	NA	5.4	2.0	1.6
4. Are you able to receive one or more Spanish-language stations clearly?					
Yes	93.2	NA	94.1	95.4	87.9
No	6.8	NA	5.9	4.6	12.1
5. Do you regularly watch television in:					
Exclusively English	13.3	NA			
Primarily English	12.3	NA			
Both equally	49.9	NA			
Primarily Spanish	12.7	NA			
Exclusively Spanish	11.1	NA			
Don't watch television	0.7	NA			

5a. What kinds of programs do you watch on Spanish-language television? [Ask of people who report that they watch Spanish television]

5a1. News	Latinos %	Anglos %	Spanish %	Both %	English %
Yes	85.5	NA	95.0	87.1	60.8
No	8.7	NA	2.1	8.1	24.0
Sometimes	5.7	NA	2.9	4.8	15.2
5a2. Dramas					
Yes	45.6	NA	57.6	45.8	21.6
No	46.0	NA	37.4	43.9	71.2
Sometimes	8.4	NA	5.0	10.3	7.2
5a3. Situation comedies					
Yes	58.1	NA	63.5	60.8	37.6
No	30.7	NA	26.1	28.1	49.6
Sometimes	11.1	NA	10.4	11.1	12.8
5a4. Sports					
Yes	58.1	NA	59.3	62.0	40.0
No	33.2	NA	32.4	29.3	50.4
Sometimes	8.7	NA	8.3	8.7	9.6
5a5. Movies					
Yes	54.9	NA	68.0	54.9	29.6
No	32.5	NA	22.0	31.7	56.0
Sometimes	12.6	NA	10.0	13.5	14.4

	Latinos %	Anglos %	Latinos who Watch		
			Spanish %	Both %	English %

5a6. Soap Operas

	Latinos	Anglos	Spanish	Both	English
Yes	52.0	NA	68.9	50.5	25.6
No	40.3	NA	23.7	41.0	69.6
Sometimes	7.7	NA	7.5	8.5	4.8

6a. Approximately how many hours of Spanish-language television do you watch each day? Please consider both weekdays and weekends in your answer?

	Latinos	Anglos	Spanish	Both	English
None	16.1	NA	0.8	2.0	57.7
Less than 1 hour	12.8	NA	10.8	11.5	17.3
1 - 3 hours	49.3	NA	51.9	62.6	21.2
4 - 5 hours	12.5	NA	19.1	15.0	1.5
Greater than 5 hours	8.3	NA	17.0	7.9	1.2
Don't Know	0.9	NA	0.4	1.0	1.2

[Ask if answer to question 5 is "Exclusively Spanish," "Primarily Spanish," "Both languages equally."]

6b. Do other adult members of your household also watch Spanish-language television or do they watch English-language television or a combination of the two?

	Latinos	Anglos	Spanish	Both	English
English	21.4	NA	22.8	20.8	NA
Spanish	26.0	NA	38.6	20.0	NA
Both	43.6	NA	24.5	52.7	NA
No other adults	9.0	NA	14.1	6.5	NA

7a. Approximately how many hours of English-language television do you watch each day? Please consider both weekdays and weekends in your answer? [Anglos asked total television watched]

	Latinos	Anglos	Spanish	Both	English
None	13.0	0.7	42.3	4.4	2.7
Less than 1 hour	13.7	6.7	18.3	12.5	11.9
1 - 3 hours	49.8	48.0	30.7	57.4	52.7
4 - 5 hours	13.4	25.7	3.7	15.6	18.1
Greater than 5 hours	8.7	18.8	2.1	9.1	14.2
Don't Know	1.3	0.0	2.9	1.0	0.4

[Ask if the answer to question 5 is "Exclusively in English" or "Primarily in English"]

7b. How about other adult members of your household, do they also watch television in English, or do they watch Spanish-language television or a combination of the two?

	Latinos	Anglos	Spanish	Both	English
English	56.5	NA	56.0	NA	NA
Spanish	11.9	NA	11.6	NA	NA
Both	23.9	NA	23.6	NA	NA
No other adults	7.7	NA	7.7	NA	NA

	Latinos %	Anglos %	Latinos who Watch		
			Spanish %	Both %	English %

8. Who do you most commonly watch television with, if anyone? [LISTEN AND RECORD]

	Latinos %	Anglos %	Spanish %	Both %	English %
Alone	36.3	36.1	41.1	31.3	41.5
Spouse	20.0	34.2	24.1	16.8	22.3
Children	11.7	12.4	11.6	12.1	11.2
Family	27.1	10.4	18.3	33.7	22.7
Other relatives	1.7	2.0	0.8	2.8	0.4
Friends	2.2	3.5	3.3	2.0	1.5
Coworkers	-	1.2	-	-	-
Other	1.0	0.2	0.8	1.4	0.4

[Ask of respondents who report that they have children in the household in the screener question 9; Otherwise skip to question 11]

9. Do the children in the household watch TV by themselves or with an adult family member?

	Latinos %	Anglos %	Spanish %	Both %	English %
By themselves	28.3	24.0	33.6	26.8	27.2
With adult family member	40.5	27.4	34.5	45.0	35.4
Both	28.6	45.2	28.6	26.2	34.0
No Answer	2.6	3.4	3.5	1.9	3.4

10. Do your children watch more English-language television, more Spanish-language television, or roughly equal amounts of each?

	Latinos %	Anglos %	Spanish %	Both %	English %
More English	71.4	NA	58.4	66.5	91.8
More Spanish	4.7	NA	10.6	4.5	0.7
Equal amounts	21.5	NA	26.5	27.5	4.8
No Answer	2.4	NA	4.4	1.6	2.7

11. Some people claim that there are not enough educational programs for children on Spanish-language television. Do you strongly agree, somewhat agree, somewhat disagree, or strongly disagree with the claim that there are not enough programs for children on Spanish-language television?

	Latinos %	Anglos %	Spanish %	Both %	English %
Strongly agree	56.5	NA	56.4	61.6	46.5
Somewhat Agree	16.1	NA	15.4	16.4	16.2
Somewhat Disagree	5.9	NA	8.3	5.7	3.8
Strongly disagree	3.7	NA	2.1	5.0	2.7
Don't know [Volunteered]	17.9	NA	17.8	11.3	30.8

12. Now I have a question about English-language children's television. Do you feel that there are positive Latino role models for Latino children on shows that they watch on English-language television? [Anglos asked about positive role models for children]

	Latinos %	Anglos %	Spanish %	Both %	English %
Yes	37.4	60.3	31.5	42.0	33.8
No	34.1	24.0	28.2	34.7	38.5
Not sure	28.5	11.0	40.2	23.4	27.7
Don't know what they watch	-	4.7	-	-	-

	Latinos %	Anglos %	Latinos who Watch		
			Spanish %	Both %	English %

13. Do you watch news programs on television?

Yes	93.4	89.4	97.1	96.4	93.4
No [Skip to 14]	6.6	10.6	2.9	3.6	6.6

13a. Do you watch the news exclusively in Spanish, primarily in Spanish, primarily in English, exclusively in English, both languages equally?

Exclusively Spanish	24.4	NA	50.4	24.0	11.6
Primarily Spanish	13.1	NA	18.1	15.5	5.8
Both languages	37.4	NA	26.0	49.2	19.9
Primarily English	11.7	NA	3.1	8.1	23.7
Exclusively English	13.3	NA	2.4	3.3	39.0

13b. When the English-language news show that you watch most frequently presents news about Hispanic men, what is the most frequent topic? [LISTEN AND RECORD] [Ship if exclusively Spanish in 13a]
See Table Four on page 73

13c. When the English-language news show that you watch most frequently presents news about Hispanic women, what is the most frequent topic? [LISTEN AND RECORD]
See Table Four on page 73

[Skip to 13e, if the answer to question 5 is "Exclusively Spanish"]
13d. Thinking about the English-language news program that you watch most frequently, does it have a Latino anchor or newscaster?

Yes	39.9	31.9	38.1	40.9	38.8
No	52.8	50.1	47.6	51.5	56.5
Not sure	7.3	18.0	14.3	7.6	4.7

13e. Do you believe that the quality of news coverage of the Latino community improves when a news program has a Latino news anchor or newscaster?

Yes	67.6	NA	73.1	69.5	58.7
No	20.5	NA	13.7	20.8	26.4
Not sure	11.9	NA	13.2	9.7	14.9

13f. Would you say that the news show that you watch most frequently presents a very positive, somewhat positive, somewhat negative, or very negative view of Latinos and the Latino community?

Very positive	29.8	17.5	38.0	30.2	20.7
Somewhat positive	34.7	38.5	30.8	36.5	34.7
Somewhat negative	19.0	10.2	14.5	19.2	23.1
Very negative	8.1	1.7	7.7	7.0	10.7
Not sure	8.4	32.1	9.0	7.0	10.7

	Latinos %	Anglos %	Latinos who Watch		
			Spanish %	Both %	English %

[Skip to 14c, if the answer to question 5 is "Exclusively Spanish"]

14. Do you regularly watch television comedies or dramas on English-language television?

Yes	57.1	66.6	30.6	56.6	71.5
No [Skip To 15a]	41.0	32.4	62.7	42.4	27.3
Not sure	1.9	1.0	6.7	1.0	1.2

14a. How common is it on these programs to present Latino characters?

Always	7.2	6.2	-	7.9	7.9
Sometimes	42.1	61.9	32.0	40.2	47.6
Never [Skip to 15a]	41.9	21.6	46.0	45.4	35.4
No Answer [to 15a]	8.9	10.3	22.0	6.5	9.0

14b. Do these Latinocharacters present a positive, negative, or neutral image of Latinos?

Positive	39.6	43.9	46.7	43.8	33.0
Negative	15.7	7.2	13.3	14.6	17.5
Neutral	44.7	48.9	40.0	41.6	49.5

14c. What is the most common image of Hispanic men in entertainment programs on English-language television?
See Table Four on page 73

14d. What is the most common image of Hispanic women in entertainment programs on English-language television?
See Table Four on page 73

15a. Now, I would like to ask you some questions about commercials that you see on English-language television. How common is it for commercials to present Latino characters?

Always	4.2	2.5	2.9	5.5	2.7
Sometimes	29.8	35.1	22.8	31.1	33.8
Rarely	34.5	40.3	26.6	36.6	37.7
Never [to 16a]	22.4	8.7	23.2	23.0	20.4
Don't know	9.1	13.4	24.5	3.8	5.4

15b. Have you ever bought a product specifically because an advertiser has used a Latino actor or a Latino character in a commercial to sell that product?

Yes	17.9	NA	17.3	20.3	14.0
No	80.4	NA	81.6	77.9	84.1
Not sure	1.7	NA	1.1	1.8	1.9

| | Latinos | Anglos | Latinos who Watch | | |
			Spanish	Both	English
	%	%	%	%	%

16a. Recently, there has been a controversy concerning a commercial presenting a Spanish-speaking Chihuahua in a starring role. Are you familiar with this commercial?

Yes	69.9	86.1	53.9	69.9	84.6
No [to 17]	29.0	12.9	44.4	29.1	14.6
Not Sure	1.1	1.0	1.7	1.0	0.8

16b. Some people say that commercials featuring the Chihuahua are insulting Latinos. Others say that the commercials are funny? What do you think? Are these commercials insulting or funny?

Insulting	12.9	5.4	14.2	14.6	9.5
Funny	68.3	76.4	69.4	65.8	71.6
Both	10.8	4.8	9.0	11.2	11.3
Not sure	8.0	13.4	7.5	8.4	7.7

[Ask if answer to question 5 is "Primarily in English," "Both languages equally, or "Primarily in Spanish," otherwise skip to 20]

17. Do you think that there is more sexual content on Spanish-language television or on English-language television, or do you think that they are about the same?

More on Spanish TV	11.1	NA	9.3	10.3	16.0
More on English TV	33.2	NA	27.9	34.7	32.8
About the same	48.1	NA	44.2	50.7	41.6
Not sure	7.6	NA	18.6	4.4	9.6

18. How about violence? Do you think that there is more violence on Spanish-language television or on English-language television, or do you think that they are about the same?

More on Spanish TV	9.0	NA	10.9	8.7	8.0
More on English TV	35.3	NA	31.0	35.2	40.0
About the same	51.6	NA	48.8	54.1	44.8
Not sure	4.1	NA	9.3	2.0	7.2

19. Some people say that Latinos are more likely be presented as being violent on English-language television than on Spanish-language television. How do you feel about this? Do you strongly agree, somewhat agree, somewhat disagree or strongly disagree that English-language televisions presents Latinos as more likely to be violent than does Spanish-language television?

Strongly agree	36.6	NA	41.1	36.4	32.8
Somewhat Agree	24.1	NA	14.7	24.8	31.2
Somewhat Disagree	14.4	NA	14.7	14.3	14.4
Strongly disagree	16.7	NA	12.4	18.2	15.2
No Answer	8.2	NA	17.1	6.3	6.4

	Latinos %	Anglos %	Latinos who Watch		
			Spanish %	Both %	English %

[Ask if answer to question 5 is "Primarily in English," "Both languages equally", "Primarily in Spanish," or "Exclusively in Spanish," otherwise skip to 22]

20. Some people have expressed the concern that Spanish-language television presents a negative image of Latinos. Others claim that the images of Latinos presented on Spanish-language are positive to Latinos. What do you think? Does Spanish-language television present a positive, negative, or neutral image of Latinos?

	Latinos	Anglos	Spanish	Both	English
Positive	45.8	NA	56.0	41.6	43.2
Neutral	31.8	NA	22.0	35.8	34.4
Negative	14.5	NA	10.4	16.0	16.0
Not sure	7.9	NA	11.6	6.5	6.4

21. Some people say that English-language television simply perpetuates negative stereotypes of groups such as Latinos, others say that television builds bridges between peoples. What do you think, does television perpetuate negative stereotypes or does it build bridges between groups in society?

	Latinos	Anglos	Spanish	Both	English
Perpetuates negative stereotypes	27.7	20.8	24.5	27.1	36.0
Builds bridges	27.6	41.3	24.1	29.5	26.4
Some of each	22.8	20.5	17.0	25.0	25.6
Not sure	21.9	17.6	34.4	18.4	12.0

22. Do you recall seeing a television program or programs that stereotyped Latinos?

	Latinos	Anglos	Spanish	Both	English
Yes	32.3	25.5	22.4	32.5	41.2
No [to 25]	49.0	59.4	53.5	50.7	41.5
Don't recall [to 25]	18.7	15.1	24.1	16.8	17.3

23. Did you see this program on English-language television, Spanish-language television, or have you seen programs with stereotypes on both English and Spanish television?

	Latinos	Anglos	Spanish	Both	English
English TV	54.6	NA	39.2	51.2	67.3
Spanish TV	9.5	NA	25.5	8.6	2.9
Both	36.0	NA	35.3	40.1	29.8

24. When people see stereotypes on television, they react in different ways. Some people stop watching the program, others protest in some way, and still others continue to watch the program. How about you, what did you do when you saw a Latino stereotype on television?

	Latinos	Anglos	Spanish	Both	English
Stopped watching	49.2	21.7	59.3	50.0	43.0
Protested	6.8	1.9	5.6	8.5	4.7
Continued watching	37.2	65.1	27.8	36.0	43.9
Other/not sure	6.7	11.3	7.5	5.5	8.4

	Latinos %	Anglos %	Latinos who Watch		
			Spanish %	Both %	English %

25. Thinking now about the presentation of Latinos on television generally, including news, entertainment, commercials, movies, etc. How would you characterize the portrayal of Latinos on a scale of 1 to 100, with 100 being very positive and 1 being very negative.

	Latinos	Anglos	Spanish	Both	English
Average	61	61	68	61	56

26-28. Please tell me the total yearly income received by you and other members of your household in 1997. Please include all income from such sources as work, social security payments, rent, interest, and anything else. What was your total income in 1997 before taxes?

	Latinos	Anglos	Spanish	Both	English
Under $9,999	9.3	3.9	14.1	9.5	4.6
$10,000 - $14,999	11.5	4.7	14.5	13.3	5.4
$15,000 - $20,000	12.6	4.7	13.2	13.9	9.6
$20,001 - $30,000	17.1	11.8	12.4	20.2	15.4
$30,001 - $40,000	11.0	14.7	5.8	10.9	16.2
$40,001 - $50,000	4.3	10.7	2.1	3.6	7.7
More than $50,000	10.2	27.2	6.6	5.9	21.9
Refused	23.8	22.2	31.1	22.8	19.2

[Ask of respondents who reported that they were born in the continental United States in Screener 6]

29. What part of Latin America or the Caribbean do you trace your ancestry to?

	Latinos	Anglos	Spanish	Both	English
Mexico	64.1	NA	56.2	75.4	78.3
Puerto Rico	15.7	NA	20.0	10.1	4.3
Cuba	3.1	NA	3.8	2.9	-
Dominican Republic	0.9	NA	1.5	-	-
El Salvador	0.9	NA	-	1.4	4.3
Other Central America	2.2	NA	1.5	4.3	-
South America	4.5	NA	5.4	4.3	-
No Answer	8.5	NA	11.5	1.4	13.0

Notes:
"NA" — Not asked.

For New York and Florida interviews, "Hispanic" was used instead of "Latino."

Latino Advocacy:
The Numbers Game

Chon A. Noriega

The Latino advocacy of the last year has in many ways been unprecedented. But it also comes after nearly two decades of deregulation and legislative dismantling of civil rights efforts. As such, it is worth looking back at the rules of engagement that have lead us to the present moment. After all, those who do not learn from the past are condemned to repeat it—on television!

In June 1993, the U.S. Commission on Civil Rights held meetings in Los Angeles as part of a multi-year study on the rise in ethnic and racial tension in the United States. These meetings responded to the resurgence of racial violence in major urban centers, addressing police-community relations, equal employment opportunity, economic development, and access to social services. Upon closer examination, the investigation marked a significant reorientation of the racial paradigm, insofar as the hearings followed upon "civil disturbances" in predominantly Latino-populated communities. The Los Angeles hearings had been planned before the riots; and, in fact, Chairperson Arthur Fletcher acknowledged that separate hearings were to have been held on Latinos in the media, since Latinos are much more underrepresented than other minority groups relative to their population. But, Fletcher explained, these hearings had been stopped by "powerful people on both sides of the aisle in Congress" who represented the interests of the film and television industry. As a result, a day of panels on television was incorporated into the commission's ongoing investigation when it met in

99

Los Angeles. Below is an account of my own testimony which surveys the previous two decades and which also questions the "numbers game" that is held up as the prerequisite for social change in a democratic, free market society.

Testimony

Since the commission's last report on minorities in television, *Window Dressing on the Set: An Update* (January 1979), three developments must be taken into account. First, networks have had to compete with cable, pay TV, and home video—within a shrinking national economy. Conventional wisdom holds that these factors are responsible for the subsequent failure to diversify primetime content and formats. I will show that this is misleading. Second, the Federal Communications Commission (FCC) has supported deregulation of television, with the result that seldom, if ever has a station lost its license for equal employment opportunity violations. Given these two factors, the commission's 1979 report still applies today. Third, we are currently at the onset of a structural change in the television industry, with multimedia technologies predicted to supplant both cable and over-the-air broadcast. These much-heralded changes do not bode well in terms of access for the non-profit sector: public groups, education, independent producers, artists, and—even—government.

In short, there is an urgent need to ensure that civil rights and equal employment opportunity are part of the communications "superhighway" of the twenty-first century. Notice that no one is calling this new entity a "freeway"—it is a commercial venture—even though its infrastructure will no doubt be underwritten by government and its revenue will derive in part from already-diminished education and library budgets. There exists a similar need to examine the Latino population, which will become the largest minority group in the same time period. For the issue at hand, however, the problem can be broken down into three major areas: audiences, portrayals, and employment.

Audiences
In a Nielsen study commissioned by Spanish-language networks Univision and Telemundo, researchers discovered weekly primetime HUT (homes using television) levels of 61

percent for Latino families, compared with a 54 percent average for the entire market. Latinos watched an average of 58 hours of television a week, compared to 47 hours a week for all viewers. The fact of a strong minority audience base often leads community and media activists to expect the television industry to exhibit some level of responsibility for this market. The change that has occurred, however, comes not from producers but from advertisers, whose expenditures directed at Latinos have grown 20 percent in recent years. After all, Latinos spend nearly $200 billion on consumer goods each year. In a sense, these figures argue against change, since the Latino population is shown as a pre-existing market that already displays the desired characteristics for profit: it is large and urban, has strong product loyalty, and watches a lot of television. Thus, these figures help networks sell commercial time and create an impetus for both minority-specific and integrated commercials but do little to facilitate other changes.

Portrayals

Latinos comprise about 10 percent of the U.S. population but have been featured in less than 1 percent of the continuing roles in primetime television series and even less in major films. In addition, these few roles appear in limited formats (situation comedies, action films) and depict characters with lower-status occupations. Between 1957 and 1987, whites played 94 percent of television's educated professionals and business executives, while Blacks played 5 percent, and Latinos only 1 percent.

Employment

Actors. A recent report by the Screen Actors Guild and American Federation of Television and Radio Artists noted that women, minorities, older people, and the disabled are vastly underrepresented on screen in comparison to their actual numbers in society. In short, no portrayals, no employment!

Directors. According to a recent Directors Guild of America report, the number of days worked by Latino directors increased from 1.0 percent of all television and film work in 1983 to 1.3 percent in 1991. As Director Jesus Trevino notes, at this rate, it will take 300 years for Latinos to reach parity with current national demographics. In this eight-year period, Latina directors worked a total of 27 days (roughly, 0.0001 percent of available work).

Writers. Minority screenwriters account for 4 percent of the guild's membership, with Latinos accounting for 0.7 percent. For all minorities, employment increased by no more than 1 percent between 1987 and 1991. Again, at these rates, it will take over 100 years for minorities to reach demographic parity. The pay gap for racial minorities is 79 cents for every dollar earned by whites, and employment is often limited to situation comedies.

Production Executives. In 1968, the Kerner Commission drew attention to the need to diversify the management level as the crux for change within the industry. A quarter of a century later, little has changed. The 1989 Hollywood Writers' Report reveals that minorities make up 1.3 percent of all primetime executive and co-executive producers and 1.6 percent of all producers and co-producers. The number of minorities in hyphenate positions (writer-producer) has remained constant at about 5 percent over the past decade. In film studios, only 2.5 percent of production executives are racial minorities.

Plus ça change

The more things change, the more they stay the same. According to the guilds, Latino employment has declined between 1998 and 1999: from 4.0 percent to 3.5 percent for actors, and from 3.1 percent to 2.3 percent for directors. Latino writers for primetime television account for just 1.3 percent of positions. Roughly 60 percent of networks and studios do not employ any Latino executives. There are no Latino executives in creative decision-making positions in the entire industry. Latinos enter the twenty-first century with a lower level of access and representation than when social protests first raised the issue in the 1960s.

The Numbers Game

While the figures for portrayal and employment have flatlined, minority populations continue to grow faster than the rest of the nation. The Latino population in particular doubled both in real numbers (from 9.1 million to 20.1 million) and as a percentage within the total U.S. population (from 4.5 percent to about 10 percent) between 1970 and 1990. Today Latinos make up 11.5 percent of the population. Nearly two and half times as many Latinos are fighting for the same percentage of jobs in the industry. As a consequence, actual employment opportunity has decreased by 50 percent since the 1970s! But since film and television are businesses, minority under-representation is often explained as a result of the need for a "universal appeal" that will satisfy a national (i.e., white) market. Minority themes and characters are seen as too much of a risk factor. But consider that about 75 percent of new television series are cancelled in their first year. In other words, following formats and actors with proven "track records" fails to achieve a "universal appeal" three out of four times. By their very nature, prime time television and feature films are high risk enterprises; so it is not a question of whether the industry takes risks but of who it lets do so.

These contradictions reveal one thing about the numbers game: it's fixed! Thus, the game becomes an impossible first step toward (1) obtaining the rights and protections already written into the law and (2) the supposed opportunities or "level playing field" of the free market system. After my testimony, I found myself questioning the commissioners themselves, asking if we really needed to prove that minorities were both underemployed and underrepresented in the media. In other words, did we really have to continue playing the numbers game, or could we move on to the practical steps that would solve these problems? Looking back at the past thirty years, progress has been the product of protests, boycotts, and takeovers more often than governmental regulation. As a consequence, progress has also been sporadic and piecemeal. No doubt, the next federal report will identify many of the same problems that it did in 1979, again calling for additional data with which to bolster its critique of the FCC and the regulatory process. Unfortunately, this assumes that the statistical substantiation of discrimination will reform the film and television industries once that information is brought to light. It will not because it has not. In the final analysis, the numbers game is more a strategy of power than a search for knowledge: its real function is to delay and disperse the demands being made by minority communities. What numbers "mean"—that is, the impact they have—depends on the power relations within which they are asserted, and without organized and sustained protest, they will mean nothing.

The Makers Speak Out

A Program for Change:
Latino Media into the Next Millennium

Ray Santisteban

Zapatistas routinely send electronic communiqués from the jungles of Chiapas. Simultaneously, on CNN, we see Iraqi tracer bullets light up the sky as American and British forces bomb Baghdad—again. Any cursory look at television today routinely demonstrates that the long prophesized age of global communications is clearly upon us. Yet, within this exciting and wondrous technological realm of modern mass communications, for a great many people of Mexican heritage, one overwhelming question resounds: Where are all the Chicanos?

The simple answer is, we are everywhere, in substantial and ever-increasing numbers. Today, we can be found in such previously unheard of places as Arkansas, Georgia, and New York.

Not only are we on the move geographically, but in cities throughout the nation, we are flexing our political muscles and taking names while doing it. Ask Bob Dornan.

But in the increasingly important field of media, Chicanos are still largely unseen and unheard—not the "sleeping giant" of politics but the "invisible man" of film.

Some believe the new millennium will bring an apocalyptic end to all humanity, thereby subverting the need for a substantive discussion on the future. But as a surviving and realistic people, we can be sure Chicanos will still be around after the year 2000—and will still be missing from mainstream television and Hollywood films.

As the nation's Chicano and Latino communities look toward both the numerous challenges and myriad uncertainties the next century will bring, there is, I believe, a compelling need to look back at what we have thus far achieved as a people in the field of media and to take stock of where we are in this increasingly important area of modern communications.

As the countdown to the Millennium continues, we should take a few moments of this ebbing century to give some thought to what our legacy has been, where it is today, and where it might possibly be going amid the innumerable potential futures that now lie before us.

THE PAST: For Sale or Rent: U.S. Archives and the History of La Raza

Since the late 1800s, much of modern history has been recorded on film and, more recently, video; these are some of the most expensive and technologically based recording instruments ever created. With Chicano cinema's recognized emergence only beginning in 1967 with Luis Valdez's *I am Joaquin*, there was a hell of a lot that happened in between that was not filmed by Chicano producers but was routinely covered by mainstream news gathering organizations.

The end result of this lack of a media production apparatus within our own community has been that a sizable amount of invaluable Chicano history is today sealed away in the storerooms and vaults of archive houses throughout the nation with limited access, excessive use fees, and worst of all, no ownership.

Chicana writer and filmmaker Elizabeth Martinez recently confronted the predicament of this legacy while producing a low-budget video version of her celebrated book, *500 Years of Chicano History*. When Martinez attempted to attain rights to use the Chicano archival photographs on which much of her book is based, she often found herself faced with the exorbitant film and photo use fees of non-Chicano archives. The situation was not one she will soon forget. "It was definitely offensive to be told by someone who was not Latino that we had to pay $250 to use one picture about racism against Latinos. It was offensive because they were making money off of our history, selling these photographs to people, and yet they were not going to give some kind of break to people whose history that is."

Yet, the question of ownership, access, and authorized use could quickly become an even more complex issue than merely paying a fee for the use of archival materials, however outrageous the fee might be.

Paul Espinosa, a veteran producer of PBS programming who most recently was Senior Producer on the 1998 three-part PBS series, *The US: Mexican War 1846–1848*, foresees a myriad of potential problems looming ahead, not just for Chicanos but for all communities who do not own their recorded historical legacy.

"The issue is 'what kind of information does the public not have access to?' because it's all being controlled by very private concerns," says Espinosa. He cautions, "You could foresee a scenario where some major conservative group would buy up all of Dr. Martin Luther King's materials with the sole purpose of never allowing anyone to use it. What happens then?"

Already the prices for the use of the material is so prohibitive that it effectively shuts out much of our community from ever seeing, researching, or utilizing these important historical resources—effectively cutting us from our own recorded past.

Although there are low-cost and even free archival materials available at some archives, most network and private archive licensing fees can run to around $2,700 for a minute of material, an exorbitant price that does not include transfer fees and tape stock.

To preserve Chicano- and Latino-produced material already in existence and help ensure that future film productions remain in the hands of our own community, we must initiate strategies that both increase our own capacity to record current events (which will become the history of tomorrow) and begin to preserve the film, video, photographic, and audio historical legacy in existence today. A comprehensive plan to this process might include the following:

• Emphasis on the recording of current community events and personalities by Raza filmmakers: We need to begin to record local events and community histories, not necessarily for their inclusion in a particular film/video but, primarily, as a way of preserving our own historical memory as a people.

• Archiving of film/video material already in existence: Filmmakers who have already produced films on subjects concerning the Latino community should think about donating copies of the raw material and research of the production to local community or academic institutions.

- Creation of partnerships between community filmmakers and local community institutions such as universities (particularly Chicano- or Latino-oriented degree programs) and historical societies: These usually are stable institutions, have trained librarians or archivists, and are not necessarily solely motivated by the desire for profit.
- Digitization of important historical films and videos: The digitization of film and video is arguably the most important development in the archiving of media, which allows for long-term storage with imperceptible image degradation. Although important for old films, the initiation of this process is particularly crucial with video formats whose shelf life is estimated at a mere twenty to thirty years.
- Consideration of legal/political approaches to the restitution of historical film material to communities: When the networks recorded stories in our communities, they immediately carted them away to their stations and eventually into their archive vaults, in effect severing these events and their long-term memories from the communities in which they were recorded. Just as the international community has adopted guidelines for the restitution of cultural artifacts stolen or expropriated from their countries of origins, efforts should be made to ensure the return of important film-based historical materials to communities from which they were taken.

These are just some ways in which our communities can begin the process of preserving and affirming our cultural/historical heritage as recorded on film and video formats. If Chicano communities are to maintain and strengthen our distinct cultural identities in a country intent on our complete assimilation, it is imperative that we begin to take steps at preserving, analyzing, and controlling our own history. The inescapable fact of the matter is that without reminders or reinforcements, memories (cultural or otherwise) fade over time. In an age where many of our Raza have embraced the self-denial and mediocrity of the term Hispanic, it is all the more important to remember a time when many of our people were proud to call themselves Chicanos.

THE PRESENT: Small Format Video: Building Chicano Cinema Today

One of the major problems our community faces, as it struggles to gain a foothold in the field of film and video production, is an overall lack of funds and training necessary to produce programs within the extraordinarily expensive field of media. Most PBS 1-hour documentaries cost $350,000 and "low budget" Hollywood films cost between five million and eight million dollars. Because of these steep production costs, I often find that most of the Chicano filmmakers I know are not spending as much time worrying about making their bad-ass definitive Chicano epic as they are in making the rent.

Austin-based filmmaker Robert Rodriguez showed the nation what $6,000 and a passion for film could do when his 1993 film *El Mariachi* burst on the independent film scene. But the real story behind the "instant success" of Rodriguez was the twenty other films he made before he garnered acclaim with *El Mariachi*.

The first projects were not films at all, they were home videos. By utilizing a consumer-brand small-format video camera (his father's) for shooting, and two VCRs for editing, Rodriguez was able to produce a series of short home movies, developing the complicated visual language of the medium that is essential to effective storytelling in films. By the time the concept for *El Mariachi* came along, Rodriguez had gained the wherewithal, training, and confidence to make the film that became the sensation of 1993.

I recall the example of Rodriguez because I believe his home video past holds the long-term solution to the perpetual curse of raising funds and the persistent lack of access to equipment that is the quagmire of the independent film producer.

Small format 8mm, VHS, and the higher cost (but still consumer-based) Hi-8 and digital video cameras are relatively inexpensive, easy to use, and readily available throughout the nation. These factors, combined with their broadcast image quality (particularly digital cameras), in my opinion make small format video the ideal medium for the Chicano community to build the in-the-trenches experience that is imperative to becoming good filmmakers in other video, and even film formats.

Not only can one learn basic video production techniques quickly, but in the process of doing so, students can produce final projects that are enjoyable, educational to watch, and even broadcastable. Although they are inexpensive, these small cameras can capture a strong video signal (especially under certain lighting conditions). Today almost all cable and public television stations are willing to broadcast these formats, as are the major three networks (though to a lesser extent).

Among these formats, digital video in particular has begun to gain international recognition as the format of independent filmmakers of the future. Several of 1998s standout films were shot in digital video and later transferred to 35mm film. These once shunned formats are increasingly becoming standard broadcast formats, largely because of their low production costs.

Unfortunately, as an instructor of video production classes for youth, I've found that new filmmakers often complain about being trained on these small format consumer recorders, impatient for access to the more professional film formats like 16mm and 35mm film.

My answer to them is based on my experiences as both an undergraduate film major at New York University (NYU), where film production equipment (particularly 16mm) is everywhere, and as a video production instructor at the University of Wisconsin, Madison. It was at NYU that I learned very quickly from both my classmates and myself that you can make bad films in any format. Because of the particular ease of the video production process, my students at Madison, however, who were taught solely in video, learned more about storytelling and more fully developed their visual language skills than most of the people with whom I went to school.

While many potential filmmakers waste precious time dreaming of making their 16mm films but not having the money to do them, they could be spending that same time learning and improving their basic production skills on small format video cameras. The democratizing effect of access to small format cameras and their low-cost, post-production counterparts, home computers, will, I believe, yield a great many of the next generation of Chicano and Latino media producers.

THE FUTURE: Cyberbarrio: Raza Producers Enter the Digital Domain

For Chicano and Latino media makers wrestling with the persistent lack of access to various media production, distribution, and exhibition venues, no new medium offers as much potential or presents as many possible obstacles as the rapidly developing world of the Internet. Developed in the 1960s as a quick and inexpensive means of sending and retrieving information within the academic community, the numerous national and international computer networks that make up the Internet have unquestionably become the most dynamic, new communication apparatus since the telephone.

Chicano and Latino media producers, some out of necessity and others by choice, are taking this general Internet use a step further. For them, the Internet's electronic transmission capabilities and low operating costs have not only created an important new tool for video production and distribution but also provided an inexpensive new means of advertising and even exhibiting their videos and films on an international market.

Los Angeles-based Pocho Productions, helmed by Lalo Lopez and Esteban Zul, in collaboration with New York-based Alex Rivera and his Animaquiladora Productions, have produced several award winning, broadcast-quality short videos using the Internet as the primary component of the production process.

These media artists, on two coasts of the nation, have created exciting new video shorts like *S16: Día de la Independencia* (a spoof of the sci-fi hit *Independence Day*), *Signs of the Times* (a critique of current anti-immigrant political rhetoric), and *Cucaracha Toonz* (animated versions of Lopez's syndicated *La Cucaracha* comic strip) by simply transferring and manipulating images, audio, and text files over the Internet. In 1997, these combined works were awarded the "Best Experimental Film" award at the San Antonio CineFestival.

Briefly, the process begins in Los Angeles, with Lopez sending still images over the Internet to Rivera in New York using the Quick Time movie software program. The images arrive within minutes, at which time Rivera will download the file and divide the images into moveable sections (for example, the antenna of Lopez's Cucaracha character). When this stage is completed, Rivera will animate the material using computer animation software and then send this now-animated version back to Lopez in Los Angeles.

Lopez completes the process by adding sound effects, music, and titles. When both feel the video is complete, the final Quick Time video file is sent once more over the Internet to Rivera who then transfers the now-completed work to the broadcast-quality Beta SP format for final tape duplication or broadcast.

According to Rivera, the collaboration, which originally began out of necessity (to save money on faxes, telephones, postage, and airfare) could easily take place between media producers on an international level. Says Rivera, "Lalo and I are working between New York and Los Angeles, but we might as well be working between New York and Mexico City, or Lima and Moscow, it could be any set of locations that have those connections."

The costs for each collaborator in this process to purchase the start up electronic gear necessary to produce these videos was approximately $4,000, a one time price that includes a computer, programs, and modem.

Although some producers are accessing the Internet as a means to facilitate video production, media activists and cultural critics are increasingly using cyberspace as a way to present information, screen video and audio clips, and advertise alternative videos through Internet-based interactive Web sites.

The Revolution Will Be Digitized (http://www.actlab.utexas.edu/zapatistas/movies.html) was produced and directed by master's candidate Tamara Villareal Ford out of the Advanced Communications Technology Lab (ACTLAB) at the University of Texas, Austin, to provide an important space for people to engage in dialogue and access hard-to-find information about the Chiapas uprising, thereby undercutting efforts by the Mexican Government to isolate and censor Zapatista-oriented information.

"The media doesn't reproduce the Zapatista's entire communiqués or the reports . . .," says Ford. "They'll just mention what happened in a sentence. On the Internet you can have an entire report or communiqué from the Zapatistas so readers have access to the whole text, or you can get a lot of background information that you can't get from other media."

In addition to presenting important resource material, Ford's Zapatista site, often referred to simply as "Zapnet," incorporates five Quick Time video clips, taken from alternative videos on the Zapatistas and their struggle. "Zapnet" also functions as an inexpensive video exhibition and distribution site by presenting brief (approximately 30 seconds) Quick Time video clips that can be downloaded and screened on any computer with Internet access and the appropriate screening programs. By providing these preview clips, along with purchase information for the full-length videos, the site encourages its visitors to learn more about the Zapatistas' struggles from progressive media productions.

The Revolution will be Digitized announces the "Zapnet" Web site, and as the examples here clearly demonstrate, the Internet is an important new way for Chicanos and Latinos to create and present alternative views and continue in the long tradition of oppositional media that has been a hallmark of both Latin American and Chicano Cinemas, which have, at times, used established media systems to produce programs for La Raza.

As the Internet continues to become a more integral part of national and international communications, it will be the challenge of Chicano and Latino media producers, and the communities from which they come, to find methods to both increase the level of access necessary to keep up with the educational opportunities that the Internet provides, and to find creative methods to use existing Internet-based technology to further give voice to our community's concerns.

Not an Academic Subject:
Latino Media Aesthetics

Frances Negrón-Muntaner

Benevolent market researchers, political analysts, and other potentially dubious characters no longer fear to announce in pointer presentations and on glossy magazine covers that Latinos will become—others say already constitute—the largest minority group in the United States. Most U.S. residents who identify as Latino are predictably elated at the joyous fertility and immigration trends that have made this occurrence possible, and eagerly await the precise moment in which a zero on the right will mean significantly more than nothing. From the way many are expecting *el cambio*, it must surely be accompanied by the South's relocation to the top half of Mercator's map; a new state of affairs of *el mundo al revés*, where *los últimos*—at last!—*serán los primeros*. Or, maybe not the first, but ahead of all the (ethnic) Others.

I am not fully a fugitive from this euphoria but *cuidado*. Living in La Florida, a small, bilingual, and ocean-front piece of real estate conveniently located between the United States and Latin America has taught me that Latino identity politics—when, where, and how it happens to flourish—is predicated on a pragmatics (strategies to achieve tangible results) and a poetics (loose structure of discourses and practices) that demand our attention to both appreciate its potential and address its limitations. Giddy or not, waking up to smell the *Bustelo* is only one way to start the day.

Latinos: More Than Thin Brown Wallets?

Due to the globalization of capital, people, and culture, never before today has it been more convenient to embrace "Latino"

117

as an enjoyable transnational strategy to remap América. While processes of market expansion and political consolidation have resulted in the Americanization of Latin America, continuous migration into the United States, internal shifting of community settlement patterns, and transnational commodity culture is also Latinizing *El Norte*. An intriguing, yet currently unanswerable, question posed by both tendencies is whether a shared bicultural public sphere will emerge throughout the Americas or whether Latinos will be fundamentally mobilized as consumers, inadvertently underscoring the gang's allegedly unassimilable "nature."

Suitably, "Latino" identities tend to have at least two incongruous ethno-national referents. First, the country of origin, where "Latinos" must be converted into a socially viable aggregate—national subjects—and then be dismissed as *los ausentes*. Second, the actual country of residence, where "Latinos" refer to perennial, foreign-born ethnics, even if U.S. born for several generations. Hence, in affirming that being Latino is *lo mejor de los dos mundos* (a formulation that status quo politics in Puerto Rico had claimed for Islanders much earlier than Telemundo did for U.S. Latinos), communities are demanding full political and economic integration to the United States, while retaining an alter/native culture—a resignification of the debate's historical parameters. After so much hunger, having the cake and eating it too is a reasonable expectation, although it raises interesting digestive questions, not to say, complications.

Although communities remain identified in specifically ethnic terms (Mexican-American, Tejano, Puerto Rican, Cubano), the national currency of empowerment—and exploitation—is "Latino." For non-Latinos, the category allows them to simplify their cognitive operations, remain in blissful ignorance over the country's colonial past/present, and classify a diverse group under a seemingly transparent category. For Latinos, the term universalizes key demands within the racialized idiom of American politics, while it masks that "Latinos" do not constitute a coherent cultural, political, or economic block. In sum, deployed within the field of politics, the investment in this category is fundamentally linked to the need to create a Subject of politics—for if Latinos do not exist, the communities so misnamed would be unable to effectively challenge the state and corporate structures. Although hysterically fragile—let's hear it for "Latino!"—the category does the job. To an appreciable extent.

At the same time, while the jury is out regarding the long term impact of Latinization, it is perhaps more entertaining to witness how the movement of bodies continues to operate more than cosmetic changes on U.S. capital(s). Not only are Latinos pushing and pulling the poor old *pellejos* of Anglo America, the demographic changes are relativizing the hegemony of single Latino ethnic groups in historically pre-occupied regions. New York, for instance, long a Puerto Rican stronghold, now shares the landscape with an increasing number of Dominicans and Mexicans, an occurrence even registered by anti-Latino graffiti: "Dominicans: The Worst Puerto Ricans." Florida, long a synonym of the Cuban *exilio*, is home to hundreds of thousands of Puerto Ricans settling in Orlando and Broward County, who increasingly make sure that the number of *boricua* flags at the Calle Ocho Festival outnumber every other kind by at least 5 to 1. If the possible links between the diverse populations that respond to the call of Latino were strictly political, however, the category would probably not hold. Here is where the heavy gravy of enjoyment comes in handy. For there is a poetics—a reservoir of signs, colonial memories, and wanderings—that allows the most diverse groups to party butt to butt in the streets of New York and with our bodies—style, voices, pleasures—continue to make ourselves fully at home in America. In this sense, "Latinoness" has much in common with cinematic representation: not necessarily false, but basically untrue.

Aesthetics: What Difference Looks Like

The building blocks of film as a multi-million dollar industry, also known as "entertainment," are synthesized in words such as markets, demographics, and deals. The operative slogans by executives, marketing departments, and producers are "deliver the audience" and "show me the money." Although Latinos have participated in the industry from its inception, Hollywood has not been the only lingo of pleasure and possibilities for spectators and filmmakers. There are other ways that Latinos have passionately made and spoken about film over the last four decades. These other conversations have taken place in festivals, cultural centers, and universities; in the realm of strategies, social construction, genre, and community building. This is, of course, the classical territory of "academics," "critics," and "activists." The rallying cry of the symbolic warfare waged by these communities ironically brings Coca-Cola to mind: "We are the real thing."

Regardless of what side of this border you stand on—or, perhaps most accurately, straddle over—discussions on Latino media aesthetics should not be dismissed as the possibly unintelligible part of a conference in which specialized professors come up with previously unheard ways of making the old new, the arcane relevant, and the unremarked absolutely essential to collective survival. Historically, aesthetic discourse refers to a critical practice through which art objects are constituted, framed, reproduced, and consumed as if they were free from pragmatic considerations. Specifically, critical discourse on aesthetics refers to the engagement with film as a symbolic practice, often supported by the analysis of particular works, through terms such as beauty, purity, and form. To paraphrase Susan Sontag, the critic's objective has been to show what it is that it is, and how it is what it is. The bottom line, however, lies elsewhere.

Although within a specific juncture one may find it strategically expedient to address aesthetic questions as defined above, it is increasingly more pressing to ask to which communities a film is what it is, and under what circumstances was it made, distributed, and accessed. By refusing to bracket the work's context of production, its historical specificity, and reception, critical activity takes a position in the struggle for—and over—culture. In a broader context, to indulge in a conversation on Latino aesthetics—and I'm thinking of the "Tres Leches" ice cream that Haagen Dasz created for the Cuban sweet tooth—is not only a pursuit necessary to accumulate the right number of juried publications for tenure, but one of the ways that cultural identity is produced as specifically Latino—or Cubano. In other words, during the paradoxical experience of watching (or tasting) the "same" film, yet processing it differently, there is an engagement with our emotions, intelligence, and cravings that constitutes one of the many ways we imagine ourselves as part (or not) of a community, be it ethnic, national, and/or racial. Within these exchanges, Latino spectators invent themselves through the ways that they articulate, present, defend, and promote the narratives—and fantasies—each lives by and for. And this process may well be a subject of the academy, but its implications are not academic.

To defend a specific aesthetics is never a purely intellectual activity. Instead, it constitutes a public struggle over the legitimacy—or hegemony—of a way of life. As Pierre Bourdieu once cautioned: "Aesthetic intolerance can be terribly violent." Think of zoot suits, loud colors, exposed underwear, and big butts and you'll get the idea. Within the marketplace and the academy, the defense of an aesthetics is also linked to upgrading Latino cultural knowledge to a socially desirable competence, increasing its market value, and assuring that the product is available for popular consumption. For instance, Latino-themed commercial cinema represents a space where Latinos get paid to perform themselves (rather better these days), although the parameters of representation may still be caught in someone else's set of rhetorical questions about Latin Lovers, Sexy Mammas, and other Spics. Through the commodification of the image and its profits, Latinos also become a "universal" value, measured in dollars. As if this was not enough, the persistence of "Latino product" can facilitate—or disrupt—group cohesion, and help consolidate the basis for political claims and economic gain. Folks don't argue over images for nothing.

The dominant approaches to film—star-centered, auteristic, as an art object or industry product—can suggest radically different political investments. The emphasis on filmmakers implies an interest in effecting change in the conditions of production; making careers viable is one of its discernible aims. Emphasis on stars shifts the attention to the spectator and his/her fantasies, and what is of importance to viewers. To see Latino films as aesthetic objects has been in part a strategy to "elevate" to the realm of form a film practice that is often perceived by dominant culture as simply a reflection of life produced without craft or mediation. In this last resignification of value, questions of meaning and knowledge allow Latino academics to carve a niche for themselves in the increasingly compartmentalized world of higher education. Each of these ways of framing the context of seeing, constitutes the difference between watching *Selena* (1997) as a film by Gregory Navas (auteur), a Jennifer Lopez movie or a Selena video (two divergently complementary fan investments), a Hollywood musical melodrama (critic), and/or as a product of "Hispanic Hollywood" (trade insider). Highlighting one or another approach is ultimately a way of signaling what's important to the speaker: creative agency, pleasure, knowledge/power, or power period.

In this sense, it is ultimately less important to call a cultural "product" Latino, than to interrogate how is it that an image, narrative, and/or style signifies "Latino" culturally and politically at a given moment (for diverse communities), and how can cultural production expand the realms of agency for audiences hailed as such. Curiously, the most complicit spectators in fashioning Latino images as authentic are after all Non-Latinos, who are more prone to see images of the group as transparently representative, particularly if these are in sync with dominant social discourse. Hence, the weight of "Latino" as a radical proposition is not to be measured in its homogenizing effect but in its ability to constantly morph into new shapes, resisting even the good-intentioned attempts to speak in its name.

Remix: Latino Media Aesthetics

Lillian Jiménez, foremother of Puerto Rican critical thinking in cinema, commented that: "While interests [among Latinos] can be similar, there are no aesthetics that bind." Indeed. Debates on aesthetics are one of the ways that the category of Latino can implode from within, as different aesthetics imply different ways of seeing, relating to, and experiencing the world. Yet, it is not so much the "content" of the conversation that constitutes many of us as citizens of the Latino State of Aesthetics (add that star to the flag!), but our participation in the act of dialogue itself. It is not what is said but the rituals of enunciation that ultimately create the effect of a common project. For "we" know that Latino aesthetics is a constructed object of study. Regardless, "we" come together ritualistically to affirm—or even deny—its existence and in the process write our will to visual pleasure as different Latinos—but Latinos still.

The transnational, multi-racial, and trilingual promise of "Latino" aesthetics creates a potentially broader context for all groups, as each claims the other's production as his or her own. In transcending the individuality and national "origin" of the producers, cultural artifacts are transformed, cannibalized, and re-contextualized to suit contemporary ends, by several generations of cultural consumers. Within this cannibalistic paradigm, it is less important to canonize—order in a clear hierarchy of importance and relevance—than to nurture the omnivorous impulse and vibrancy of contemporary Latino cultures. It is less important to formulate paradigms, than to understand the multiple forces that constitute and undermine Latino possibilities—and limitations. So, while we will often read that a suspiciously large sample of Mexican-American films are concerned with music and the border, Cubans with the Castro regime, and Puerto Ricans with affirming cultural nationalism, these classifications overlook those experimental, intimate, and autistic cinemas that interrogate, displace, and even disrupt hegemonic accounts of its own delight.

Latino cinematic space is where Latino subjectivities are mobilized into fantasy and play—social and sexual. Yet, this is not a transhistorical phenomenon, and there is much discrepancy concerning its effects. Hence, while it is arguable if a film by a Tejano named Robert Rodríguez can be considered "Latino" in the same breath as one made by a chorus of Jewish men such as *West Side Story*, it is the argument itself through which Latino spectatorship is constituted, affirmed, and enriched. Ironically, as we argue over a Negra Modelo (a beer, that is), one can discover how ethnic identification, such as the one that occurs when children insist that Morticia and Gomez Addams are really Cuban, receives a poetic confirmation when Angelica Houston plays a Cuban lady in *The Perez Family* as well as Morticia herself alongside the late Raul Julia. The fact that Lt. Torres in the Roddenberry series *Voyager* is clearly a Klingon, is stereotypically consistent with the fact that everyone is well aware that Ms. Torres is 100% Klingo-Rican.

Raving about a fabulous performance or researching the details of a specific director's life does not exhaust our conversation. Noting whether a production has a big or peewee budget belies the question of signification. We know the language of moneyed aesthetics: stars, color-coordinated wardrobe, air-blown hair. We also recognize a certain aesthetics of poverty: people with the sex appeal of your next door neighbor, K-Mart slacks, and hair blown by the cars screaming by. However, lack or abundance does not entirely dictate the uses of resources, nor whether the more expensive choices actually manage to take the audience along for a ride. For, is *Desperado* a better picture than *El Mariachi*? To whom? Under what conditions? Or is the truly consequential question, indisputable: What's the movie with Salma Hayek in it?

Your turn.

Fractured Fables from Latino USA:
A Primer on Experimental Media Arts

Rita Gonzalez

> If the smog is not too severe when you stand atop
> nearly any rooftop in Los Angeles, you can see the
> Hollywood sign as it beckons to the world with its
> multibillion-dollar myth. When you climb back down
> into your own backyard and walk along the streets,
> everything can be considered a façade, everyone can
> be acknowledged as an extra, and you can be the
> brightest-burning star.
>
> —Harry Gamboa, Jr.

The first Latino Producers Conference, held in early June
1999, made possible the gathering of numerous generations
of makers, critics, and supporters of Latino media. During
one of the conference's many lively panels, video artist Alex
Rivera presented a cross sampling of emerging producers.
Rivera characterized the works of this—his own generation—
as strongly connected to and informed by popular culture
and political currents. Genres are melding as the trans-
disciplinary approaches of the visual and performing arts fuse
with the identity-based politics that informed documentary
film and video practice throughout the 1980s and 1990s.

Those filmmakers who are approaching mainstream industry productions are doing so with self-consciousness and levity.
Through the powerful vehicles of satire and parody, writers and
directors (such as Rivera, Esteban Zul, Ela Troyano, and Juan
Garza) find it possible to comment on the longstanding subsid-
iary positioning of Latinos in commercial film and television. On
the outskirts of the industry lie experimental productions.

The following alphabet of Chicano and Latino makers seeks to broaden the term *experimental* beyond a limited reading that has been conceived mostly in reference to an Anglo-European avant-garde tradition, from Cubism to Situationism. The inclusivity of this experimental list seeks also to bridge gaps across the visual and media arts, following the recent wave of Chicano and Latino makers coming out of contemporary arts training (from Guillermo Gomez-Peña to Iñigo Manglane-Ovalle).

ASCO (and also After-ASCO, and also for the Society for the Preservation of ASCO founded by members of ALARMA[1]). Chicano Counter Cinema was born when Los Angeles-based artists Harry Gamboa Jr. and GRONK conceived of the first Chicano film about plastic, dysfunctional families, and the condition of urban exile.[2]

Also for *Animación*—Makers like Sergio Arau, Renee Moreno, Felipe Galindo, Frances Salomé España, Alfonso Alvarez, and Alex Rivera prove that some of the most formally innovative work is taking place in the realm of animation. Inspired in equal parts by graphic traditions of political poster art from Latin America, the international manifestations of experimental animation, and pop cultural icons like *The Simpsons*, the new wave of animation expresses itself through allegory and pastiche.

Border art. The ongoing critical dialogue on borders includes not only metaphorical discourses on the body, but a wealth of visual art and criticism about the tensions between geographic designations and transnational cultural flows. The dynamic zone of the U.S. and Mexican border has been remapped in the works of David Avalos, Louis Hock, Liz Sisco, ERRE (Marcos Ramirez), Berta Jottar, Jesse Lerner, and Ruben Ortiz-Torres.

Curators con visión. Innovative curators (some of whom double as filmmakers and/or scholars) like Sergio de la Mora, Jimmy Mendiola, Ray Santisteban, Karim Ainouz, Berta Sichel, C. Ondine Chavoya, Jennifer Maytorena-Taylor, Euridice Arratia, Christina Ibarra, and Fred Salas have featured emerging makers and fostered a wide array of aesthetic practices. By constantly situating the work of emerging makers against that of the first Chicano and Latino makers and Latin American filmmakers, these curators have enhanced the understanding of the aesthetic and practical transformations characterizing media production of the 1980s and 1990s.

Documentary (undone) *al estilo Portillo*. Lourdes Portillo, Mexicana/Chicana maker, has pioneered a poetic and visually innovative approach to documentary. Since the 1970s, Portillo's work has fused intimate portraiture with political resolve. Her powerful film *Madres de Plaza de Mayo* (19xx) raised international awareness of the organic activist movement started by the mothers of the disappeared in Argentina. Since the more structurally traditional works of Portillo's early period, she has redefined the rules of documentary observation through her keen impulse and spontaneity. *El Diablo Nunca Duerme* (19xx) perhaps went the farthest into her personal history but turned out to be less about the Portillo familial web and more a portrait of secrecy and repression in Latino cultures. Her work has had a strong influence on documentary makers from Jimmy Mendiola (*Pretty Vacant* [1995]) to Jennifer Maytorena-Taylor and Vicki Funari (*Paulina* [1997]).

Emerging Makers. Veronica Majano, Manuel Solis, Alfonso Alvarez, Aldo Velasco, Lisette Barcellos, Maya Tilman-Salas, Charlotte Gutíerrez, Ana Saldaña, George Reyes, etc, etc., etc.

Festivals. Over the past two decades the Guadalupe Arts Center's CineFestival, San Diego Latino Festival, and Cine Acción's Cine Latino have done the most to foster experimental work on both regional and transnational levels. Consistently providing mainstream Latino makers an opportunity to test out grass-roots methods of distribution, the directors of the aforementioned festivals have nevertheless accommodated the true diversity of genres and production values.

Gamboa, Harry. Last year, influential film scholar Chon Noriega brought to light Harry Gamboa Jr.'s scripts, interviews, poetry, performance pieces, and essays, proving that Gamboa is not only a maverick maker of socially conscious and diametrically oppositional (to the "official" Chicano aesthetic) videos and photographs, but also one of the most wildly innovative writers of our time.

Hispanics in Hollywood. The first Latino experimenters? Narrative film emerged from what has been described by silent film scholar Tom Gunning as a cinema of attractions. Long before Hollywood's steady and slight stream of narrative forms, silent short spectacles featured dancing and careening exotica that had been features of World's Fairs and vaudeville stage shows. Dark writhing bodies have always made good fantasy. Think back to the first experimental Latino performers (and here I include the mimetic strains of Laurel and Hardy speaking Spanish phonetically in their early serials for the Latin American film market). Lupe Velez left her career as cabaret performer in Mexico City for a career in Hollywood. In the popular RKO *Mexican Spitfire* series, she acted misrecognition, imperfect diction, and performed what the Surrealists would have called *automatic speaking*. And years after they left their indelible images on celluloid, Carmen Miranda and Maria Montez provided the subversive contents of much of queer aesthetics.

Installation. New technologies are utilized by a growing number of Latino installation artists to address the interplay of language and power (Daniel J. Martinez), the construction of racial types via the sciences (Iñigo Manglane Ovalle), and the dynamism of popular cultural expressions and politics (Ruben Ortiz-Torres and Alex Rivera).

Joyas del Kitsch. Maria Montez/ Mario Montez, Pepon Osorio, Los Super Elegantes, Ela Troyano, Carmelita Tropicana, Laura Alvarez, Nao Bustamante y Las Cucas, Coco Fusco, Luis Alfaro, Cholita, *Pocho Novela* (Coco Fusco and the Chicano Secret Service), ALARMA, and Pocha Peña.

Latin American and Mexican makers in dialogue with U.S. based Latinos. Over the last decade, film festivals throughout the Americas have witnessed a growing dialogue between U.S.-based Latino and Latin American producers. For the last two years, binational conferences have been taking place in Mexico City during the *Festival del Cortometrajes* exposing Latinos to the important works of Roberto López, Julian Hernandez, Paulina del Paso, Miguel Calderón, Grace Quintanilla, and many others.

No Movies. ASCO's low-fi strategy to make art-making as affordable as a cup of coffee at Phillipes.

Orbital indecision y otros originales. *My Trip in a '52 Ford* (1966) by Ernie Palomino; *Mozo: an Introduction into the Duality of Orbital Indecision* (1968); *Requiem 29* (1971) by David Garcia.

Pochismo. Esteban Zul and Lalo Lopez are as transgressive as they want to be and are now at work on a (anti) Hollywood film that has been described in some circles as the *Kentucky Fried Movie* for the 1990s.

Also Cine de Papas (a variation on the Aesthetics of Hunger—making videos on potatoes, nearly for the price of potatoes) and its founder Alex Rivera (*Papapapá, ¿Why Cybraceros?*, and his most recent masterpiece *Papas del Papa*).

Queer cinema. Perhaps the most critically attuned works are those that speak from a subject position always under scrutiny and constantly transforming. Queer makers are intersectional and critical thinkers who balance and tip the plates of personal narrative with an assemblage of interrogations of social space and political alliances. Among these makers: Raul Ferrera Balanquet, Jennifer Maytorena-Taylor, Frances Negrón Muntaner, Augie Robles, Al Lujan, Osa Hidalgo, Charlotte Gutíerrez, Aurora Guerrero, and Paco Francisco Valasquez.

Raphael Monatañez. He took part in the FLUXUS movement by tearing pianos to shreds and producing filmic collages. The event was recently reprised a year ago at a contemporary art museum in Los Angeles as part of the large-scale exhibition *Out of Actions*.

Super 8 filmmaker Willie Varela. He moved through his hometown El Paso as flaneur with a camera capturing the gentle and difficult moments of a life lived through film.

On a personal note: *Stacatto Purr the Exhaust* by Luis Meza and *Selena* by Gregory Nava (the split-screen concert footage an obvious homage to Kenneth Anger)—My two favorite Chicano experimental feature films!

Tejano...puro Tejano. Jimmy Mendiola's *Pretty Vacant* might have just created the Tejano boho aesthetic, but it also provided a guidebook on the innovators of Chicano subculture (from Los TeenTops to Los Bros. Hernandez to The BRAT). The coolest Chicano experimental film ever made!

Underground Puerto Rican filmmaker Jose Rodriguez Soltero. His films of the 1960s have been rediscovered by scholars and curators in the United States. Soltero's film *Lupe* (1965) was screened two years ago at MIX NYC experimental film and video festival as part of a tribute to his collaborator Mario Montez.

Video Pioneers. Gustavo Vasquez, Willie Varela, Edin Velez, Lourdes Portillo, and Frances Salome España.

Ximena Cuevas' videos. sophisticated slices of life in Mexico City that blend the intimate micro-melodramas of her everyday life with astute observations about the country where she was born and raised. Recently, Cuevas has been working in dialogue with U.S.-based video artists Bonita Makulich and Melody Calvert on notions of the American dream in the states and in Mexico.

Y *Zone Four*. Perhaps the world's first Chicana prison movie from Osa Hidalgo, the genre bending maker of *Olmeca Rap* and *Marginal I's*.

Notes

1. ALARMA (Artists in Los Angeles Reconfiguring Media Arts) is a renegade group of chola-centric critics and artists. The ensemble has produced the videos *st. francis of aztlán* and *The Assumption of Lupe Velez*. Their *Manifest(o) Destiny* lists their twenty-six point plan to (finally) end the folkloric impulse in Chicano art.

2. See the interviews between the two artists recently reprinted in *Urban Exile: Collected Writings of Harry Gamboa Jr*, edited by Chon A. Noriega (Minneapolis: University of Minnesota Press, 1998).

Notes from the
NALIP Conference

Generation EXiled—*No Mas*

The New Generation of Latina/Latino Filmmakers and Producers

Fabiola Torres

A new generation of Latina/Latino filmmakers and producers are caught between the anti–Vietnam war–protest–free love–civil rights–advocate generation and the teenage–lip syncing–teen idols–Pokemon–triggar happy generation. This group's experience was affected by Reaganomics, the Bush Regime, political struggles in Central America, wars for oil, increased college tuition, and race riots on urban streets. During their motion picture encounters, movies about white college kids losing their virginity, wars in space, and white Americans saving poor and helpless Third World people influenced their perspective of Hollywood. Armed with their cameras and a political conscious, these Latinos are in a battle in protecting their dignity and are fueling a new Latina/o-grassroots-centered cinema revitalization *con ganas.*

There is a reality that confronts this new generation. The majority was raised during a transitional point of America's economic structure. America went from an industrialized country to a deindustrialized global economic structure embodied by the distribution of "American" images, sounds, goods, people, media, and consumerism. In addition, anti-immigrant sediment polluted the political climate, which made Latinos an unappealing ethnic group. As a result, the basic human functions were devalued by turning people into decapitated consumers and into white American aspirants. This consumer-centered environment definitely effected the new generation. However, there was something special about their passion in film that created resistance and endurance.

133

This passion was developed in several ways. On the one hand, many gathered their inspiration from Chicano or Latino Studies courses offered in the universities, and others acquired it from the lack of representation of Latinas/os in mainstream motion pictures as they grew up. Experimental films or the very few Latino-theme movies (i.e. *La Bamba, El Norte, Mi Famila*) and artistic expressions created by Chicanas/os and Latinas/os of the 1970s-1990s inspired some, while other's found the need to release their creative voice. Many are still in school pursuing their master's degrees in creative media/arts, but others are involved in this creative movement as a hobby or a second career. Some have already produced their films and are being screened in film festivals, yet very few have obtained distribution.

The new generation is now living in a time where every market wants to ensure a large profit and global distribution. In the entertainment world, movies have to appeal to a large audience to secure profits. Confronted by this, some Latinas/os in the entertainment industry have had to use the word "cross-over" to appeal to the executives. Is that what it comes down to? Do we have to compromise ourselves to appeal to large profits? Many of the young filmmakers and producers who attended the First Annual National Association of Latino Independent Producers in San Fransisco (June 1999) said, "*¡chale!*" to that.

While the conference took a lunch break, forty to fifty young Latinas and Latinos came together in the Hilton's lobby to meet, talk, share information, and have a drink. All felt the necessity to educate one another on the issues that were being discussed at the conference. The majority was lost given all the acronyms being thrown around—NLCC, LPBP, NCLR, CPB, PBS etc—while others were still trying to understand the premise of the conference. However all felt the need to make an impact in this newly formed organization of Latina/o independent producers. They were not going to allow their life experiences to be taken for granted.

One of the key obstacles discussed among this new generation was their lack of networking skills. Because competition, isolation, and individualism hovered over them, they realized their weakness at a conference where networking was going to take place. Most of the "vanguard" present in the conference knew each other. There was lots of smooching and introductions among themselves. Many of them invited individuals from the new generation to attend the conference. Yet these young Latinas/os didn't know each other. Some attended the same universities but didn't recognize each other's ambitions in filmmaking or producing. It was a fragmented and disillusioned group with a common goal— to create visual narratives of their experiences as men and women. They realized the need to create a communal and collaborative relationship. The "vanguard" was organized and had a plan. The new generation needed a method to survive in this Latino film movement.

Several methods and strategies in creating and producing films were suggested such as having tamale sales to finance projects, while others talked about grants that apply to their projects. Also, equipment availability was shared and technological advice exchanged. In addition, dialog about practical, creative, and successful tactics were presented. To cite an example, Esteban Zul from POCHO Productions and Smoking Mirrors Production (Los Angeles) was one of the featured panelists in a workshop called "The New Generation." His movie, *The Flour Wars,* was screened and intrigued many who saw it because he made it on a $0.00 budget.

"I just called up a couple of my closest friends and people who owed me a favor (other film artists), dressed them up like indigenous people and let them run around half naked in the sun. After, we threw a raging party with free drinks and food that everyone contributed to and had a great time."

As a result, POCHO Productions and Smoking Mirrors have a good reputation in Los Angeles for throwing awesome parties. Now everyone who knows them or is associated with them wants to assist them in their projects. Smoking Mirrors is currently in demand by local Chicana/o musical bands that want a video made. Although the video shoots are not charged to the band, Francisco Hernandez, co-founder of Smoking Mirrors, can always rely on these bands, such as Aztlan Underground, Quetzal, Quinto Sol, Blues Experiment, to volunteer their services when they do fundraisers to finance their films. This exchange between a production company and friends became a successful strategy in producing a film.

All in all, they realized there are obstacles that challenge them or may be stumbled upon, but together they were going to form a cohesive, grassroots unit of collective resources that may ensure success as a group. Be it a support group or an advocate constituency, they wanted to assemble a national community of new Latina/Latino filmmakers and producers who would work together.

Although many conference goers called this group Generation ñ, the new generation refused to be defined. What started off as a social gathering (and possible organization), ended up with a well-developed networking and support prototype/model. This model became—*film@raza.org. Film@raza.org* is a list serve that is more than a directory. It is a virtual space for the group to exchange information, ask for help, share project ideas, and simply keep in touch. Some results have been people car-pooling to film festivals, housing visiting artists or producers, supplying free equipment, casting calls, job or intern opportunities, screening announcements, as well discussing the conditions of Latinas/os in the industry. Links will be constructed to affirm effective communication amongst them. Finally, they will be actively participating in the planning and developing of future conferences for NALIP.

The future is bright for this new generation. No longer will they accept their exiled status as Generation X. They are going to make films! These Latinas/os know that such mass communications methods as film shape identities and cultures, but they are not going to wait for Hollywood to open their doors. Their camera will become their weapon, their creativity will be the ammunition, *film@raza.org* at *www.raza.org* will be the soldier, and together they will be a part of a cinema revolution that will blow Hollywood away. There is no other choice because it is vital for the representation and understanding of Latinos in America. The cinema revolution will be coming to a theater near you! Brace yourself!

Rising from the Ashes:
San Francisco Conference Plots the Future of Latino Independent Media

Juan José Rivera

Hardcore film historians will tell you that there is already a Latino film movement in this country; it just doesn't get seen. The crisis within the Latino filmmaking community this past year (see *Release Print* April 1999) has forced us to ask: Isn't that the point? Why has there never been a concerted effort within the Latino community to create an organization like the Independent Feature Project, Frameline, or Film Arts Foundation—an organization that would be devoted solely to producing and distributing Latino media? If such an organization did exist, what form would it take? How should it position itself in relation to mainstream media, particularly public television? In designing a Latino media organization, what could we learn from the history of Latino filmmaking? What has our community been doing right—or wrong? And what has the mainstream filmmaking community not been doing that provokes Latino filmmakers to create their own innovative ways of producing and distributing their works? These questions and others were discussed at this summer's first-ever national conference of Latino filmmakers in San Francisco.

Billed as "The Future of Latino Independent Media: Public Television and Beyond," the conference was convened by six groups: the Coalition for Latino Programming on Public Broadcasting, the Latino Producers Ad-Hoc Committee, the

National Council of La Raza, the National Hispanic Foundation for the Arts, the National Latino Communications Center (NLCC), and the newly formed Latino Public Broadcasting Project (LpBp). The conference provided an opportunity for Latino filmmakers from across the nation, many of them frustrated by recent trends in public television, to put their heads together and plan their future—not only in relation to PBS but, more importantly, in relation to each other, independent of any government-funded agency.

The conference began to take shape last winter, when several individuals exchanged e-mails addressing their concerns over the Corporation for Public Broadcasting's (CPB) de-funding of the NLCC, the Latino component of the five minority consortia funded by CPB, and their reassigning funds to LpBp without any input from the Latino film community. (See the accompanying article by Julia Segrove Jaurigui.) Some two dozen Latino independent producers met in Los Angeles in December 1998 to discuss the NLCC issue. Despite our different opinions about the NLCC, we found ourselves united in struggling against a pronounced "disconnect" between CPB and the diverse and growing field of Latino producers. It was resolved that if CPB would not engage in a dialogue with Latino producers, then the producers should get together and talk to each other.

Bienvenida (Beni) Matias, director of the Center for Arts Criticism in Minneapolis, and UCLA film professor Chon Noriega became co-chairs of a conference planning committee. In a letter announcing the planned San Francisco gathering, they pointed to three goals: "(1) Organizing ourselves as a creative constituency; (2) taking an active role in defining our institutional needs within public television; and (3) looking beyond public television to the new media environment within which independent programming might find other outlets." The conference planners concluded, "In short, this conference now combines mentorship and advocacy with commercial and public media opportunities."

The conference took place in June, and it got off to a wonderful start. At the opening reception, conference facilitator Leticia Nieto said, "This event is already a success, and all you have to do is look around at everyone who is here and notice the fact that people have been hugging, asking each other questions—and I've seen business cards flying around. You should congratulate yourselves now because you've already succeeded!"

Nieto's remarks were encouraging, but the dismantling of the NLCC—compounded by many people's frustration with that organization—created much nervous anticipation, which was compounded by an incredibly busy agenda. Perhaps knowing what was to come, Rosalía Valencia, executive director of Cine Acción, the conference's host organization, reminded everyone in her welcoming remarks that we were in for an intense weekend. Valencia said, "I promised my friend, Ray Santisteban (from the Coalition for Latino Programming on Public Broadcasting), that I would tell all of you—Let's get ready to rumble!"

Moving Forward

Putting first things first, the conference attempted to get the NLCC issue out of the way. The participants in an opening-day panel titled "National Latino Communications Center: Lessons Learned" generally agreed that the NLCC's problems were its own fault, and that the situation it created was an embarrassment to the Latino community nationwide. But though the topic generated considerable heat, a consensus was reached that Latino filmmakers need to get past their frustrations with the NLCC, while learning from its mistakes when creating a new consortium. Later, in a "town hall" meeting, attendees decided that any new consortium representing Latino filmmakers should set term limits for its directors and board members, and should hold them more closely accountable in order to prevent their losing touch with the people they are supposed to serve. At another panel, "The Future of the CPB Minority Consortia Model," moderated by ITVS executive director Jim Yee, executive directors from other minority consortia presented working models from their own organizations.

Deciding on a new consortium to represent Latino filmmakers—and to hand out CPB money—was perhaps the most divisive issue at the conference. Some participants were adamant that LpBp, headed by actor Edward James Olmos, should run the consortium for at least one more year. Others thought that the best choice would be the Latino Programming Coalition, made up of three already established community media groups—the Association of Hispanic Arts of New York, the Guadalupe Cultural Arts Center in San Antonio, Texas, and Cine Acción in San Francisco. The discussions got heated, and no conclusion was reached as to which group would form the new consortium, but both LpBp and the Latino Programming Coalition promised to submit proposals to CPB. [LPBP was later awarded the contract.]

By the second day, conference participants were able to move on to other things. One of the most exciting topics was how to move beyond PBS and create a new member-based organization to provide Latino producers with funding, equipment, mentorship and (dare I say it?) distribution. This discussion grew out of the town hall meeting, in which those "core issues" were identified by the group as a whole. "We want to take all of the core issues and mold them into a membership organization," said New York media consultant Lillian Jimenez, one of the conference's organizers.

It was a beautiful sight to watch everyone break up into six smaller groups and work at lightning speed to develop ideas about how the "governance, function, funding, education and community, values and professional development" would work in relation to a new membership-based organization. One person from each group was selected to continue working on the vision for this Latino filmmakers organization. "This is a unique opportunity," said Chon Noriega. "We have brought 250 people together from around the country. We have the opportunity to bring the Latino production community together to take leadership. Whoever wants to can come forward and say, 'I want to play a leadership role in strengthening this community,' and make sure that a year from now we're not just having memories, we're coming together again in a new city and taking it one step farther."

The Next Generation

My favorite part of the conference occurred during an event that was not planned by the organizers. It was when "The Next Generation," or Generation Ñ, as some were calling it, met informally to get to know each other as fellow filmmakers. Prompted by the stimulating dialogue following a screening of some of their works, a group of young filmmakers decided to take it outside and just plain talk. Eventually a circle of about 40 participants engaged in a discussion in which everyone got a chance to introduce himself or herself and describe their resources and skills. It was obvious that this new generation of Latino filmmakers is dying to work with each other. "We got together and said, You know what? We're all trying to make these films, and we've been having to go to other people [to make them], but what happens when we come together despite the differences in what we like to make?" said Diana Perez of Es Tiempo Productions in Ventura County, who was chosen as a spokesperson for the Next Generation. "We realized that if we come together, between us all, we have what it takes."

True to their status as children of the new-technology age, the group compiled a long e-mail list, and Fabiola Torres from Southern California offered to put it all together and get us all hooked up electronically. No sooner had Fabi offered to do that, than Rebeka Rodriguez from Berkeley offered to put up a Web site where the Next Generation could feature their projects and network with each other. The conference participants left this gathering convinced that the future is as bright as that magical light that will project our films.

Note

This article originally appeared in *Release Print*, the magazine of Film Arts Foundation. Reprinted by permission.

Learning the Hard Way:
What Happened to the National Latino Communications Center?

Julia Segrove Jaurigui

On the eve of the 21st century, a Latino presence is being strongly felt in American music, literature, sports, music, and politics. In fact, many political strategists believe that Latinos, now some 30 million strong, and on the verge of becoming the second-largest political constituency in the United States, could swing the vote in the next presidential election. If Latinos are able to flex that kind of political muscle, why are they the most under-represented ethnic group among independent filmmakers?

Although racism is a consideration in any debate about the dearth of independently produced ethnic media in the United States, it's not the only answer in this case. For over a decade, ideological debate and well-intentioned efforts to resolve complex, thorny issues revolving around gender, class, cultural, and ethnic differences, homophobia and assimilation have splintered the Latino mediamaking community. If you add to the mix the difficulty of anybody "making it" in independent film, it's not surprising that only a handful of Latino producers have won any degree of recognition or support.

A great many Latino mediamakers claim, with good reason, that the ongoing under-representation of Latino programs on public television is in part due to the longtime failure of the National Latino Communications Center (NLCC) to meet the needs of its constituency. Starting in 1979, the NLCC functioned as the minority consortium distributing

Corporation for Public Broadcasting (CPB) money to Latino film and videomakers for the production and airing of programs on PBS. (Other CPB-affiliated minority consortia represent African Americans, Asian Americans, Native Americans, and Pacific Islanders.) The NLCC became a political football in early 1998, when CPB, alleging misuse of funds and conflicts of interest, defunded the organization.

In late 1998 the situation went from bad to just plain awful when CPB, without consulting the Latino mediamaking community, chose the Latino Public Broadcasting Project (LpBp), a Los Angeles nonprofit run by actor-indie producer Edward James Olmos, as the interim organization to replace the NLCC. LpBp was given $1.3 million to distribute in grants to Latino producers in 1999. The resulting uproar over what was perceived by many as an arbitrary decision by CPB resulted in a series of seminars in Los Angeles, San Francisco, Miami, New York, and San Antonio last spring, which were attended by Olmos, delegates from CPB and PBS, and hundreds of Latino film and videomakers. Eventually, CPB issued a call for proposals for a new group to succeed LpBp, although at this writing, none has been selected. [LpBp submitted a proposal and was selected by CPB.]

It was against this backdrop of controversy that more than 250 attendees at the first-ever Latino independent mediamakers conference pressed into San Francisco's Chinese Cultural Center on a Friday afternoon in June to get the lowdown on the CPB/NLCC debacle from members of the Latino community and industry insiders. At the conference's plenary session, titled "The National Latino Communications Center: Lessons Learned," UCLA professor Chon Noriega; filmmakers Moctesuma Esparza, Rick Tejada-Flores and Gregory Nava; NLCC representatives Raquel Ortiz and Beatriz Olvera-Stotzer; and Film Arts Foundation director Gail Silva talked for nearly two hours about the breakdown of CPB's partnership with the NLCC and the future of the Latino consortium.

In a lengthy yet sincere explanation about the events that led to the NLCC's defunding, NLCC board member Ortiz told the audience that "the NLCC did a lot of things right before it did a lot of things wrong." Admittedly, the NLCC did fund some quality, award-winning Latino projects, many of which were broadcast on PBS. But as producer-director Tejada-Flores (*Fight in the Fields*) reminded both the panel participants and the audience, the real issue under discussion was the NLCC's longstanding refusal to be accountable to the community it was supposed to represent. Veteran Hollywood producer Esparza (*Selena*), echoing Tejada-Flores's concerns, urged the audience to learn more about CPB's role in the NLCC fiasco.

Director Nava (*Mi Familia, Selena*) chided the NLCC for its failure to develop young Latino talent during the 1980s, lamenting that an entire generation of Latino mediamakers has been overlooked. NLCC treasurer Olvera-Stotzer responded that CPB did not fund the NLCC with the intention that they "act as a springboard to develop talent," and the NLCC was therefore under no obligation to "nurture" young Latino filmmakers. Since the NLCC mission statement clearly lists "training and related assistance to develop and support Latino media talent" as one of the three elements that define the NLCC's "purpose and work," Olvera-Stotzer's comments seemed, at the very least, unfortunate. Olvera-Stotzer also spoke about former NLCC executive director Jose Luis Ruiz's efforts to defend the embattled organization against ongoing rumors and allegations of "kickbacks, improper accounting procedures and embezzlement," all of which Olvera-Stotzer says have "yet to be proven by the government."

After hearing several complaints about the NLCC's inability to do its job, panel moderator Noriega reminded the audience that while it was helpful to talk about the shortcomings of the NLCC, it was also important to learn from the experience and not repeat the same mistakes in the future. Gregory Nava, a co-founder of the Independent Feature Project/West, asked the Latino community to apply the civil rights model of "principles over personality"—ensuring that a movement is driven by basic principles and not just by a leader or celebrity—when developing the new Latino consortium.

At the end of the plenary session, almost everyone in attendance was more than eager to put the unpleasant CPB/NLCC experience to rest and to take whatever steps are necessary to ensure the creation of a Latino consortium committed to both representing and working with a diverse Latino mediamaking community. Although direct mention of LpBp and Edward James Olmos, who attended the plenary, was avoided, it was clear that many members of the community were monitoring the activities of both CPB and LpBp.

The future of Latino independent media is in the hands of producers, media activists, and funders who are committed to talking, listening, organizing, and working together to build a diverse national alliance of Latino mediamakers. Given the extraordinary goodwill, energy, and steadfastness that went into presenting the Latino independent media-makers conference, it's not hard to imagine that the "good old days" lie ahead.

Note

This article originally appeared in *Release Print*, the magazine of Film Arts Foundation. Reprinted by permission.

NALIP Conference Reports

NALIP
Conference Facilitator's Report

Leticia Nieto

The following is the facilitator's report on the June 1999 conference held in San Francisco on the Future of Latino Independent Media. It details the process established for the conference to increase dialogue and move toward consensus and action.

Conference Goals

Stated Goals of the Conference

The stated goals developed by the planning committee for the conference were:

- Organizing ourselves as a creative constituency.
- Taking an active role in defining our institutional needs within public television.
- Looking beyond public television to the new media environment within which independent programming might find other outlets.

Met Goals of the Conference

I observed that the stated goals were met by the conference as follows:

Organizing ourselves as a creative constituency

- A Latino/Latina membership advocacy organization "trade" group of independent media producers (and related others) was formed.
- A vision statement for this group was drafted.
- A task force was appointed to implement the vision statement with input from the full membership.

Taking an active role in defining our institutional needs within public television

- During the conference, clarity was brought to the sequence of events and various parties' involvement in the defunding of the National Latino Communications Center (NLCC).
- Participants planning to submit responses to the RFPs from the Corporation for Public Broadcasting (CPB) had opportunities to express their intention, discuss implications, and commit to a statement of values, which the participants in the conference shared and agreed should be followed by the organization being formed.
- At the end of the conference, a delegation wrote and presented a unified statement of principle that CPB should follow in their selection process for a Latino Consortium.

Looking beyond public television to the new media environment within which independent programming might find other outlets

- Discussion about the organization included much visioning which embraced the new media environment.
- Participants in the conference found an emerging sense of their community plotting its own course to cable and other media outlets in addition to the CPB and Public Television.

Facilitation Goals for the Conference
To facilitate the processes by which the participants met the conference's goals, I had the following facilitation goals:

- Identifying voices which would need support in order to be heard.
- Creating contexts of support to empower those voices to be heard.
- Allowing the conference co-chairs and key persons to have every opportunity for forming coalition and cooperation in support of the wider membership.
- Providing focus and assisting productivity so that the conference participants would have a sense of progress toward the goals for the conference as a whole. This was a concern because the time was short, and it was clear that the conference was an opportunity not to be lost for the maximum achievement of the goals.

- Encouraging each participant to get into touch with, and to stay aware of, her or his *individual* motivations and goals regarding the conference so that each would powerfully act and speak from that place.
- Working to allow participants to integrate what *each individual* came to do and what *the collective* came to do.
- Creating conditions for leadership to emerge out of the various constituencies which made up the conference.

Description of Facilitated Conference Activities

Session: Defining Core Issues

The purpose of this session was to encourage expression of and capture the diversity of ideas about the matters of greatest importance to the participants in a new organization.

The method used in this session was a brainstorming format with a "town hall" structure. The participants were gathered in concentric circles. The facilitator and two assistants with roaming microphones elicited comments from those present. Two scribes documented and displayed the ideas that were being generated.

Phase One

The younger generation of producers was asked to speak. This worked well to bring forward new ideas and concerns that were not necessarily determined by any of the old or recent history of past agendas or events.

Phase Two

There was an effort to include everyone who wished to speak. The session was kept focused as much as possible on the agenda of considering the issues around a new organization.

Some of the challenges were that after a long day of conferencing, participants were tired. Also, in this forum, there are possible tendencies for individuals to dominate the conversation—limiting the diversity of voices, or turning the process into a debate—squelching the free flow of ideas and concerns, which are the goals of brainstorming. In the session we succeeded in creating and maintaining an open space where everyone could speak and participate in a free flow of ideas. Also, the focus was kept on a new organization, rather than on other conference issues such as the Latino consortium selection process.

The session was high energy and had a remarkable degree of participation. I believe that upwards of 90% of those in the room contributed to the process. Because there were more people with things to say than there was time available, the opportunity was created for ideas, comments, and questions to be added in writing on the large sheets of paper around the room where the brainstorming content had been documented. Also, there was a high level of resonance within the room—people were speaking what many were thinking. In addition, it was surprising that when asked about agreement on specific points, there was a high level of agreement for a group of over 200 persons.

Follow-up Phase
There were many pages of important points elicited in the session. Following the session, the facilitator and a small group sorted and reviewed all of the ideas, points, and questions which had been captured. Eight categories of comments were identified.

- Mission and Values.
- Governance—how the organization should be structured and run.
- Function—what the organization would do.
- Funding—how the organization would seek and disburse funds (other than CPB).
- Development—seeking and raising funds to support the organization itself.
- Education and Community Outreach—how the organization would advocate in these realms.
- Professional Development—mentoring and training for individuals at all levels.
- Ideas and Decision Items *Unrelated* to the creation of the organization, yet which should be dealt with in the conference.

Session(s): From Core Issues to Working Agenda
In this session, the purpose was to take the ideas generated the previous evening and to deepen them in ways that would allow the participants to move forward in achieving the most critical "next steps" while maintaining an open discussion inclusive of a variety of voices. In addition, the steps decided upon needed to reflect the will of the group as a whole. The session began in the morning, continuing into another phase during "open space" in the late morning and into the afternoon.

Phase One

The method used to deepen discussion and agreement on the issues was to break the participants into small task groups. A group was formed around each of the seven areas related to the new organization. Each group was given the task of discussing, clarifying, refining, and recommending next steps for the topic they were representing. The group was also to take notes on their discussion. The ideas generated the previous night related to the group's area were provided to the group. Facilitation was provided to each group to assist with fluidity of process and focus.

The benefits of this approach were as follows:

- While the previous night's format was brainstorming and not a dialogue, the small group structure encouraged dialogue.
- Participants had the opportunity to self-select the area in which they were most interested and to take the consideration of that topic to a deeper and more specific level.

Phase Two

Reports on the discussion of each area were provided from the specific groups to the conference as a whole.

Phase Three

A smaller group made up of two representatives from each group remained to participate in the next phase. In practice, for the rest of the day, conference participants came and went, participating as they chose in this ongoing work session.

The method used to create the next level of synthesis was a "fish bowl" technique. Two circles were formed. Only those in the inner "fish bowl" circle would actively speak in the discussion. Others, in the outer circle, were listener-participants. However, if a listener-participant wished to make a comment or otherwise enter the discussion she or he could tap the shoulder of someone in the "fish bowl" requesting to trade seats. For this application of the fish bowl technique, one was to take the seat only of another representative of the group that had discussed the same topic area in Phase One. The benefit of the fish bowl is that it allows a manageably sized group to actively participate in discussion. This keeps discussion from getting bogged down, and at the same time makes it possible for everyone with something to share to speak and be heard in an organized and organic manner.

It emerged in the fish bowl discussion that the next task for the conference was to write a vision statement for the new organization. Another idea that emerged early in the day was that there should be a task force to take forward the vision developed in the conference. The ongoing work session using the fish bowl format refined the work of the seven small morning task groups toward an understandable document that could guide the work of the task force.

Measuring levels of agreement was handled by an approximate consensus process: if the speakers active in the fish-bowl agreed and there was an absence of additional comment by the participant-observers (who if they did have thoughts to add could enter the fish-bowl) a point was considered resolved, and the discussion progressed to the next issue. Because of the processes used in this working session, the content of the document created reflects a high level of agreement and participation from each of the small work groups, and from every constituency in the conference.

The strong agreement early on for the necessity of a Task Force also allowed certain issues where clarity was difficult to achieve to be "tabled" so that constructive work on other issues could go on. There was a high level of agreement among participants in the work session that the product of this day would of necessity contain discrepancies that would need the attention of a Task Force. For example, agreement on the question of the wording to be included in the name of the organization was elusive. Some thought the term "media" was comprehensive, others preferred "media artist," others felt that "film and television" needed to be named. In the process of the work session, it was agreed, however to leave it to the Task Force (and to take up other matters where agreement was more easily available).

Session: Putting the Puzzle Together

This session included a presentation by a small group of the vision statement to the rest of the conference participants. Copies of the vision statement were made available, and participants were encouraged to review and consider them. Accompanying the vision statement was a request that the Task Force be appointed by the conference conveners the following morning. The charge is for the Task Force to review and implement the revised vision statement.

Follow-up/Pre-planning Phase

The facilitator and conference planners met before the morning's session in order to be able to respond to the request that a Task Force be appointed. The conference planners appointed a Task Force, as requested by the membership of the conference, with attention to include diversity in membership.

Session: Resolutions and Future Steps

The purpose of this session was offer any clarification needed on any of the conference issues and topics. It was also the opportunity for conference outcomes to be outlined and acknowledged.

During this session

- The Task Force was introduced.
- An opportunity was provided for anyone additional who was interested to join the Task Force.
- The Task Force committed itself to facilitate formation of next year's conference committee.
- The Vision Statement was ratified in a unanimous vote of the conference.
- A Clarification was made as to the two applicants for CPB RFPs and their pledge to abide by the values and principles articulated in the Vision Statement.
- A delegation emerged to work on and deliver a statement of principles to the CPB.

At this point, the Conference was closed.

Session: Preparation of the Statement to the CPB

A delegation deliberated and produced a statement to the CPB. A copy of the statement is attached in the appendices.

The outcomes of this working session were the following:

- The delegation documented a statement of principle to the CPB regarding the "Latino Consortium RFP" selection process. The statement of principle was based on the Vision Statement that emerged at the conference and served to represent the membership in one voice.
- The delegation contacted Robert Coonrod, President & CEO of the CPB.
- Mr. Coonrod agreed to meet with the delegation, who presented him with the signed statement. Mr. Coonrod welcomed the statement and was visibly moved by it.

I believe it is worth noting that the Statement to the CPB has the following significance: the signatories acted and agreed to the contents of the statement
- as representatives of their own organizations,
- in coalition with the other organizations,
- as authorized spokespersons of the new organization,
- and as delegated representatives of all the attendees of the conference.

Final Observations

During the conference, the participants worked well as a group. They were able to develop agreement and to act even when faced with challenges. As the organization takes life and shape, there will need to be continued attention to empowering voices that need support in order to be heard. I believe that the organization will best be able to meet its goals and meet the goals of the members if it remains aware of the need to focus on this dynamic. One very obvious area where this need is evident is when considering the need for visible and outspoken leadership by women. Attention to these issues will be crucial to maintain the cooperative decision making begun at the conference.

Vision Statement from NALIP

We, the membership, request that a task force be appointed by the conveners of this conference to distribute, review, revise, and implement the following vision for this Latino/Latina membership advocacy organization. We ask that this task force request feedback/critique/input from the full membership and use this information to update/correct the vision statement they will implement. We wish this task force to be appointed on Sunday morning. We realize that many unresolved issues and discrepancies will need to be addressed by the task force and this membership. We offer the following vision statement as a beginning.

Mission
The mission of this organization is to promote the advancement, development, and funding of Latino/Latina film and media arts.

The goal is to foster solidarity and mentorship among its members.

Value Statement
1. Commitment to Latina/Latino media and filmmakers regardless of form or content of their work.
2. Respect for diversity based on a code of ethics open to and respectful of differences—Including gender, geography, color, class, age, ethnicity, language, sexuality, religion, genre or physical abilities.
3. Commitment to solidarity and accountability, applying our code of ethics to the selection, funding, and mentoring processes.

4. To raise the question of historical and cultural relevance and awareness of Latinos and Latinas.
5. Commitment to solidarity, alliance building, and multiple visions of Latina/Latino experiences within the local, national, international and global contexts.

Governance:
Governing Board
1. Persons in governing board (suggested 15 members).
2. Two thirds plus one—quorum.
3. Age, gender, religion, roles, language (Spanish/English) diversity in membership.
4. Three year rotation (1/3)
5. Board creates administrative structure and fills executive director and other positions.
6. Standard for effective practice. Task force discuss style i.e. consensus, Robert's rules of order, or other.
7. Accountability (checks and balances) to general membership, including public record of activity and ombudsperson.
8. Yearly conference for yearly review by membership for accountability.
9. Communicate by newsletter.
10. Electing board by agreed upon method.
11. All decision happens from the ground up—reflective of what the membership wants.

Advisory Board
8. Recognized names to serve as political and professional 'angels'.

Review Panel
1. Rotating review panel
   A. Taskforce to clarify methods for distribution of funds.
   B. Experts in the related disciplines. Task force to determine and define criteria for selecting experts.

Development
1. Self-sustaining funding structure.
2. Endowment
3. Professional grant writers.
4. Former grantees participate in fundraising for organization.
5. Organization as Executive Producer with percentage of profits.

6. Accountability.
7. Outreach to diverse sources of funding.
8. Ownership/profit sharing/commercial partnership.

The Primary Functions of the Organization are:

Production Funding
1. Equitable accountable granting program.

Advocacy
1. Industry wide.
2. Political involvement.
3. Public Policy.
4. Alliances/support (re: granting).

Serving as Producers Resource
1. Fiscal agent.
2. Directory—professional.
3. Web-site and data base.
4. Commissioning studies (stats/reports).
5. Creating opportunities.
6. Access to equipment.
7. Dissemination of information (accountability).
8. Multi-medial library.
9. Research new technology.
10. Legal support.

Distribution
1. Identify and develop distribution channels.
2. Cable channels.
3. Alternative streams.
4. PBS packaging and promotion.
5. Educational distribution.
6. Special screening.

Professional Development
The objective is to foster and create:
1. Fundraising consultantship.
2. Fiscal management workshops.
3. Encourage internships/staffing as crews for grantees' productions.
4. Marketing workshops for grantees.
5. One-on-One mentors.
6. Facility/resources.
7. Create a Latino/Latina film/TV school.
8. Explore different mentoring models (i.e. DGA).

9. Production workshops.

10. Services for artists at all levels.

Education and Community Outreach
1. Educate investors about the advantages of investing in Latinos.
2. Outreach for community through training programs "media skills."
3. Hire an educational/outreach position that connects people and identifies potential resources.
4. Create links between educational institutions and the membership.

Funding
1. Support professional productions.
2. Consider models including Sundance, IFP, etc (guidelines and bylaws for funding only).
3. Create opportunities for emerging and student projects.
4. Have funding choices be sensitive to representation of regional, genre, gender, sexual orientation and other diversity.
5. Negotiate with (apply) to CPB and others.
6. Straightforward application process, clear forms, criteria standards.
7. Administrative board separate from funding process.
8. Space out eligibility to apply for funds.
9. Hold open calls and specialized calls.

Statement to the Corporation for Public Broadcasting

We have been authorized as a delegation from a conference of over 250 film and television producers, academics, writers, media activists, and community organizations involved in media advocacy to present a statement of principle to CPB regarding the "Latino Consortium RFP" selection process.

We urge the Corporation for Public Broadcasting to use and apply the following criteria in the selection and evaluation of submitted proposals towards this RFP. Since the selected entity will be the sole disburser of funds for administrative and production support to the field, it is imperative that the process of selection be guided by the principles of accountability, transparency, and access. This can be ensured by the following standards:

1. The selected entity must be democratic in composition and governance and representative of the national constituency that it will serve.
2. Its policies, rules, and guidelines must be transparent and adhere to the values and principles ratified at the conference.
3. Access to all information, especially guidelines and selection criteria, must be made available in a timely and widely distributed manner.
4. The entity must have a demonstrated history of the following principles:
   - A commitment to Latina/Latino media and filmmakers regardless of form or content of their work.
   - Respect for diversity based on a code of ethics open to and respectful of differences, including gender, geography, color, class, age, ethnicity, language, sexuality, religion, genre, or physical abilities.

- A commitment to solidarity, alliance building, and multiple visions of Latina/Latino experiences.

<u>This communiqué is the definitive reflection of the will of the Latino/Latina national media community.</u>
This is an attempt to restore a relationship that was fractured. We have requested this meeting with you to convey the sentiments of this group and to inform you that, as a result, a new national media advocacy organization has been created. This organization represents the national field of producers, academics, media advocates, and community organizations promoting the proliferation of Latino media.

All of the organizations that announced an intention to submit a response to "Latino Consortia RFP" have pledged to adhere to and be held accountable by the guidelines and value statements agreed upon at this conference. Among those organizations are the Latino Programming Coalition and the Latino Public Broadcasting Project.

The Latino Programming Coalition consists of:
Association of Hispanic Arts
Cine Accion
Guadalupe Cultural Arts Center
National Hispanic Foundation for the Arts

The will of this conference is that the Corporation for Public Broadcasting adhere to the spirit of these guiding principles in its evaluation, final selection, and contracting process this year and in years to come. Further, it is the conference's will that these principles be communicated to our Representatives in Congress, the national media, and our constituents. We wish to further the inclusion of Latino programming to reflect our national presence and stature in American Culture in the tax-supported Public Broadcasting Service and the Corporation for Public Broadcasting.

We look forward to establishing a continued dialogue with you regarding the future of Latino independent media in the digital age.

Coalition for Latino Programming on Public Broadcasting
Latino Producers Ad-Hoc Committee
Latino Public Broadcasting Project (LPBP)
National Hispanic Foundation for the Arts (NHFA)
National Latino Communications Center (NLCC)
National Council of La Raza (NCLR)

162

Latinos in Media Directory

Latinos in Media Directory

This directory lists Latinos working in front of and behind the camera in film, video, television, and digital technologies. It also includes funders, distributors, scholars, and activists who support Latino-produced and Latino-themed work.

Maria Agui Carter
31 Crescent St. #1
Cambridge , MA 02138
Ph: (617) 354-4547
Em: mariacarter@medione.net

Carlos M. Aguilar
14104 Goleta St.
Arleta , CA 91331
Ph: (818) 891-5519

Jorge Aguirre
206 Rivington St. #3D
New York , NY 10002

Valentin Aguirre
21st Century Aztlan Productions
3356A 16th St.
San Francisco, CA 94114
Ph: (415) 255-9878
Em: tinobear@hotmail.com

Susana Aiken
Star Fish Productions
330 West 42nd
New York, NY 10036

Elvia Alvarado
314 Monterey Road #18
South Pasadena , CA 91030
Ph: (626) 441-9016
Em: ealvar83241@aol.com

Dino Andrade
Klaxon Filmworks
10853 Rose Ave #39
Los Angeles, CA 90034
Ph: (310) 836-6051
Fx: (310) 287-1149
Em: dnoandrade@aol.com

Rafael Andreu
3758 Prairie Ave.
Miami Beach , FL 33140

Alex Anton
4867 Southwest 1148 Crt
Miami , FL 33185
Ph: (305) 299-9310
Fx: (305) 225-8373
Em: Adios@bellsouth.net

Carlos Aparicio
Star Fish Productions
330 West 42nd
New York, NY 10036

Lucero Arellano
California Arts Council
1300 I St. Suite 930
Sacramento, CA 95814
Ph: (916) 322-6588
Fx: (916) 322-6567
Em: larellano@caartscouncil.com

Eddie T. Arnold
Communications Council
Nielsen Media Research
1627 K St. NW
Washington, DC 20006
Ph: (202) 296-1936
Fx: (202) 296-7908
Em: arnolde@tvratings.com

Liz Arreaga
The Backshop
1906 Sherburne Dr
Los Angeles , CA 90034
Ph: (310) 838-3885
Fx: (310) 838-3823
Em: backshopla@aol.com

Ishmael Arredondo Henriguez
P.O. Box 1481
Hollywood , CA 90078
Ph: (323) 462-5448
Fx: (323) 462-5448
Em: ishmaelh@pacbell.net

Aida Arriola
San Diego State University
522 Campaniel Drive
San Diego, CA 92182

Yoko N. Arthur
VP Program Operations
Corporation for Public Broadcasting
901 E Street NW
Washington, DC 20004-2037

Bernadette Aulestia
HBO
1100 6th Avenue
New York, NY 10026

Carlos Avila
8701 West Olympic Blvd.
Los Angeles , CA 90035
Ph: (323) 850-2895

Bruce Baca
16247 Sunset Trail
Riverside, CA 92506
Ph: (909) 789-1516
Fx: (714) 762-7795
Em: bdbaca@gte.net

Lisa Baca-Sigala
Durazo Communications
660 S. Figuero Street
Los Angeles, CA 90017
Ph: (213) 239-6555
Fx: (213) 239-6550
Em: Bacasigala@earthlink.net

Alberto Barboza
3362 Kenneth Dr.
Los Angeles, CA 90032
Ph: (323)343-9037
Em: abarboza@ucla.edu

Lisset Barcellos
158 Sanchez Street
San Francisco , CA 94114
Ph: (415) 861-2609
Fx: (415) 861-2609
Em: borderline2@prodigy.net

Mario Barrera
1422 Kains Avenue
Berkeley , CA 94702
Ph: (510) 642-9134

Germán Barrero
573 South Lake Ave. #7
Pasadena , CA 91101
Ph: (909) 920-4411
Fx: (909) 920-4416
Em: barrero@earthlink.net

Rosalinda Barrero
573 South Lake Ave. #7
Pasadena , CA 91101
Ph: (909) 920-4416
Fx: (909) 920-4416
Em: barrero@earthlink.net

Frank Barron
KOCE-TV PBS-50
15751 Gothard Street
Huntington Beach , CA 92647
Ph: (714) 895-5623
Fx: (714) 895-0811
Em: ebd@cccd.edu

Shalini Batra
Rauber Filmworks
696 10th Ave. #1C
New York, NY 10019
Ph: (212) 713-0663

Marta N. Bautis
505 E. 6 St. Apt 3F
New York, NY 10009
Ph: (212) 673-8065
Fx: (212) 673-8065
Em: mnoemi@aol.com

Alfredo Bejar
475 Washington Ave #2H
Brooklyn , NY 11238

Dalida Maria Benfield
Video Machete
2511 N. Bernard
Chicago, IL 60647
Ph: (773) 862-4932
Fx: (773) 506-9932
Em: dbenfield@artic.edu

Lori Benson
MediaRights.org
443 Broadway 5th floor
New York, NY 10013

Susan Berry
IDA
75 Spring Street # 504
New York, NY 10012

Anna Betancourt
IFMCCA DI
1840 Grand Concourse Ave.
Bronx, NY 10457
Ph: (718) 466-1000
Fx: (718) 466-1220
Em: info@ifmccadi.org

Nicole Betancourt
Nota Bene Productions
17 Thompson St. #7
New York, NY 10012
Ph: (212) 334-7235
Fx: (212) 334-7236
Em: nbprodinc@aol.com

Ismael Betancourt Jr.
IFMCCA DI
1840 Grand Concourse Ave.
Bronx, NY 10457
Ph: (718) 466-1000
Fx: (718) 466-1220
Em: info@ifmccadi.org

Tania Blanich
National Video Resources
73 Spring Street, Suite 606
New York, NY 10012

Elissa Blatteis
253 West 72nd St. #1707
New York , NY 10023

Carlos Bolado
Sincronia Productions
1442 A Walnut Street #476
Berkeley, CA 94709
Ph: (505) 525-8998
Fx: (505) 525-8919
Em: bolex@pobox.com

Piedad Bonilla
Piñata Productions & Management
1221 Horn Ave. Suite 8
West Hollywood, CA 90069
Ph: (310) 358-1943
Fx: (310) 358-0812
Em: pinatamgmt@hotmail.com

Margarita Borda
Sunshine Productions
2040 Diamond Street #4
San Diego , CA 92109
Ph: (619) 274-2034
Fx: (619) 274-2034
Em: marboda@earthlink.net

Frank P. Borres
Latino Entertainment Group
327 Red Oak Road Suite B
Bridgeport , CT 06606
Ph: (203) 372-6526
Fx: (203) 372-6526
Em: fborres@aol.com

Wendy Braitman
IFFCON
360 Ritch Street
San Francisco, CA 94107
Ph: (415) 495-2327
Em: wbraitman@iffcon.com

Giovanna Brokaw
457 South Ogden Drive
Los Angeles , CA 90036
Ph: (323) 939-3715
Fx: (323) 939-3715
Em: gbrokaw@bigplanet.com

Oscarr Bustos
2650 West Highway 33
Rexburg , ID 83440

Michelle Byrd
Independent Feature Project
104 West 29th St. 12th Fl.
New York, NY 10001-5310
Ph: (212) 465-8200
Fx: (212) 465-8525
Em: ifpny@ifp.org

Albert Caballero
Action Talent Management
6255 Sunset Blvd. # 2201
Hollywood, CA 90028

Nora I. Cadena
November 20 Productions
1812 Page Street #4
San Francisco, CA 94117
Ph: (415) 666-0205
Fx: 415)831-8934
Em: nov20@sirius.com

Hector Canonge
36-24 35th Street
Astoria , NY 11106

David Capurso
Constant Pictures/Emanon Ent.
51 Newel St. # 3-L
Brooklyn, NY 11222
Ph: (917) 748-7436
Fx: (718) 398-6446
Em: capu5@aol.com

Dennise Carignan
P.O. Box 10573
Oakland , CA 94610
Ph: (510) 234-7958
Fx: (510) 632-4718
Em: escritoria@aol.com

Tony Carrion
AHA!
250 W. 26th St
New York, NY 10001

Al Castañeda
3rd Millennium Films
P.O. Box 24726
Los Angeles, CA 90024
Ph: (818) 886-6891
Fx: (818) 886-6891
Em: al@latinoheritage.org

Marisa Castañeda
Orale
P.O. Box 667058
Houston, TX 77266
Ph: (713) 522-5369
Em: mcastan@ix.netcom.com

Richard Castaniero
208 S. Bonnie Brae #2
Los Angeles , CA 90057
Ph: (213) 483-8353
Em: cast@ucla.edu

Eloisa A. Castillo
Orale
10909 Gulf Freeway #902
Houston, TX 77034
Ph: (713) 944-3795

Harry Abraham Castillo
Mercado Corporation
11111 Santa Monica Blvd.
Los Angeles, CA 90025
Ph: (310) 914-3007

Arcie Chapa
KNME-TV
1130 University NE
Albuquerque, NM 87102
Ph: (505) 277-1242
Fx: (505) 277-2191
Em: achapa@unm.edu

Calixto Chinchilla
PO Box 1041
New York , NY 10023

Monica Chuo
Samuel Goldwyn Films
1133 Broadway # 1101
New York, NY 10010

William A. Cintron
5340 S.W. 99th Ave
Miami , FL 33165
Ph: (305)274-2608

George Cisneros
1918 W. Houston
San Antonio , TX 78207
Ph: (210) 527-0377
Fx: (210) 472-3011
Em: cisneros@dcci.com

Nicole Cox
Edge Productions
870 Market St. Suite 767
San Francisco, CA 94102
Ph: (415) 781-3343
Fx: (415) 781-3343
Em: edgecinema@aol.com

Margaret Cruz
Latina Breast Cancer Foundation
259 Monterey Blvd.
San Francisco, CA 94131
Ph: (415) 585-1163
Fx: (415) 586-7453

Tania Cypriano
37 King St. #6A
New York , NY 10014

Victor De Jesus
Passion Entertaimment
47-14 159th St.
Flushing, NY 11358
Ph: (718) 463-3441
Fx: (718) 463-3441
Em: Vdejesus@aol.com

Sergio de la Mora
355 Edinburgh St.
San Francisco , CA 94112
Ph: (415) 586-3851
Em: jalisco@cats.ucsc.edu

Angel de Leon
Mi Gente Automatic Productions
355 West 52nd St. 7th fl.
New York, NY 10019

David de Leon
Millennium Crop Entertainment
2517 12th Avenue
Los Angeles, CA 90018

Carlos E. de Martini
45 Kimball Rd.
Chelsea , MA 02150
Ph: (617) 492-2777
Fx: (617) 497-4278

Amaroq de Quebrazas
821 Head St.
San Francisco, CA 94132-2813
Ph: (415) 333-6411
Em: amaroq@sirius.com

Desi del Valle
Frameline
346 9th Street
San Francisco, CA 94103-3809
Ph: (415) 703-8650
Fx: (415) 861-1404
Em: desi@frameline.org

Margarita R. del Valle
Esparza/Katz Productions
8899 Beverly Blvd. # 506
Los Angeles, CA 90068
Ph: (310) 281-3770
Fx: (310) 281-3777
Em: chiriui@hotmail.com

Johnny Delgado
1410 Steiner St. #PH1D
San Francisco , CA 94115
Ph: (415) 345-8728
Fx: (415) 364-2367
Em: johnnydelgado@hotmail.com

Marlena Dermer
Latino Public Broadcasting
6777 Hollywood Blvd. #500
Los Angeles, CA 90028
Ph: (323) 466-7110
Fx: (323) 466-7521

Robert Diaz LeRoy
New West Crash Films
4615 Los Feliz Blvd. #1
Los Angeles, CA 90027
Ph: (323) 663-8860
Em: leroyhb@earthlink.net

Denise DiIanni
WGBH Educational Foundation
125 Western Ave.
Boston, MA 02134
Ph: (617) 492-2777
Fx: (617) 864-8539
Em: denise_diianni@wgbh.org

Alberto G. Dominguez
P.O. Box 931268
Los Angeles , CA 90093-1268
Ph: (323) 478-0367
Fx: (323) 254-1618
Em: hollywood@loop.com

Juan Dominguez
Grants for the Arts
City Hall Room 347
San Francisco, CA 94102
Ph: (415) 554-6710
Fx: (415) 554-6711
Em: juan@sfgfta.org

Claudio Duran
Interfaze
2135 Derby Street
Berkeley, CA 94705
Ph: (510) 644-1310
Em: cduran@jps.net

J.C. Duran
Evil Twin Productions
5201 Fulton Avenue
Sherman Oaks , CA 91401
Ph: (818) 986-8551
Fx: (818) 986-8582
Em: jcduran@aol.com

Armando Duron
3500 West Beverly Blvd.
Montebello , CA 90640
Ph: (323) 728-0311
Fx: (323) 728-0390
Em: duron@pacbell.net

James Encinas
Taper Forum
Latino Writers Workshop
608 7th Ave.
Venice , CA 90291
Ph: (310) 450-4814
Fx: (310) 859 2778
Em: nora@bdhc.usa.com

Judith Escalona
733 Amsterdam Ave.11F
New York , NY 10025

Maria Escobedo
43-05 242 Street
Douglaston, NY 11363
Em: Cghera1801@aol.com

Moctesuma Esparza
Esparza/Katz Productions
8899 Beverly Blvd. #506
Los Angeles, CA 90068
Ph: (310) 281-3770
Fx: (310) 281-3777
Em: esparzakatz@msn.com

Paul Espinosa
Espinosa Productions
4800 Marlborough Drive
San Diego, CA 92116
Ph: (619) 284-9811
Fx: (619) 220-6895
Em: espinosa@electriciti.com

Sonny Espinoza
3655 Westwood Blvd. #5
Los Angeles , CA 90034
Ph: (310) 280-0259
Em: sonnye@ucla.edu

Natatcha Estebanez
The Blue Diner Film Project
121 Lewis Road
Belmont, MA 02478
Ph: (617) 484-1325
Fx: (617) 484-2383
Em: natatcha@aol.com

Anne Etheridge
Bay Area Video Coalition
2727 Mariposa St.
San Francisco, CA 94110
Ph: (415) 558-2183
Fx: (415) 861-4316
Em: anne@bavc.org

Evelina Fernandez
Sleeping Giant Productions
5911 Allston St.
Los Angeles, CA 90022
Ph: (323) 887-0665
Fx: (323) 887-9600
Em: slgiant@aol.com

Olly Fernandez
10920 Wilshire Blvd #150
P.O. Box 9115
Los Angeles, CA 90024
Ph: (310) 274-3197
Fx: (310) 274-3298
Em: tshirt776@aol.com

Louis Fernando Hernandez
Fiddler Productions
852 First Ave. South
Naples, FL 34102
Ph: (941) 435-1818
Fx: (941) 435-1168
Em: fiddlerpro@aol.com

Sean Ferry
1538 Waller Street
San Francisco , CA 94117
Ph: (415) 863-5767
Fx: (415) 863-5702
Em: sean@bomze.com

Frank Figueroa
Continental Airlines
7300 World Way West
Los Angeles, CA 90045
Ph: (310) 258-3513
Fx: (310) 258-3545
Em: ffigue@coair.com

Noemi Figueroa
El Pozo Productions
76 De Haven Drive #5F
Yonkers, NY 10703
Ph: (914) 969-0118
Fx: (914) 969-0118
Em: figgeeys@aol.com

Pablo Figueroa
CemiCircle
321 West 22nd St. #48
New York, NY 10011
Ph: (212) 243-4383
Fx: (212) 243-4383
Em: cemicircle@erols.com

Beatriz Flores
El Taller
1236 Curtis St.
Berkeley, CA 94706
Ph: (510) 527-4166
Fx: (510) 527-4166
Em: medusa@flash.net

Vicente Franco
Franco Productions
12 Liberty Street
San Francisco, CA 94110
Ph: (415) 282-3069
Fx: (415) 282-1798
Em: vefoio@ige.org

Rosa Linda Fregoso
818 Santa Ray
Oakland , CA 94610
Ph: (530) 754-7525
Em: rlfregoso@ucdavis.edu

Vicky Funari
CineMamá's Productions
156 Wool Street
San Francisco, CA 94110
Ph: (415) 285-0517
Fx: (415) 552-8979
Em: vix@sirius.com

Hector Galán
Galán Productions Inc.
5524 Bee Cave Rd. # B-5
Austin, TX 78746
Ph: (512) 327-1333
Fx: (512) 327-1547
Em: galan@galaninc.com

Moses Galindo
559 Palisades Drive
Pacific Palisades , CA 90272
Ph: (310) 573-0058
Em: mogalindo@earthlink.net

Federico Gambo
1516 Buena Vista #203
San Antonio, TX 78207
Ph: (210) 212-8942

Alicia Gamez
29 Lapidge #1
San Francisco , CA 94110
Ph: (415) 703-0378
Em: agamez@leland.stanford.edu

Jose Jesus "JJ" Garcia
Garcia Motion Pictures
6505 Mobud Drive
Houston, TX 77074
Ph: (713) 661-4042
Fx: (713) 779-7016

Irma Garcia- Sinclair
Syngarnicity
P.O. Box 791
Alameda, CA 94501-8791
Ph: (510) 522-1182
Fx: (510) 864-3222
Em: syngar@earthlink.net

Juan Garza
6256 Church Street
Los Angeles , CA
Ph: (323) 478-9505
Fx: (323) 478-9505

Thom Geier
The Hollywood Reporter
1515 Broadway 12th fl.
New York, NY 10036

Devora Gomez
Dar Luz Films
9542 ½ E. Oak St.
Bellflower, CA 90706
Ph: (562) 804-4516
Fx: (562) 804-4573
Em: darluzfilms@aol.com

Greg Gomez
NLAE MI
8899 Beverly Blvd. #506
Los Angeles, CA 90048
Ph: (310) 281-3770
Fx: (310) 281-3777
Em: gomez@latinomedia.org

A.P. Gonzalez
6312 Gilday Drive
Los Angeles , CA 90068
Ph: (323) 957-1936
Fx: (323) 957-1938
Em: apg@ucla.edu

Adriano Gonzalez
14460 ½ Dickens St.
Sherman Oaks , CA 91423
Ph: (818) 986-8777
Fx: (818) 850-8777
Em: adriano@pacbell.net

Hector Gonzalez
Ramparts Productions
3745 W. 58 Street
Maywood, CA 90270
Ph: (323) 589-4626

Marco Vinicio Gonzalez
El Diario
345 Hudson St
New York, NY 10014

Martin Gonzalez
P.O. Box 1734
Santa Monica , CA 90406
Ph: (310) 664-9707
Fx: (310) 664-0909
Em: buddha2001@aol.com

Omar Ezequiel Gonzalez
CaloCine
6230 Wilshire Blvd. #70
Los Angeles, CA 90048
Ph: (800) 786-0747
Em: omar@calocine.com

Rita Gonzalez
725 S. Spring Street #22
Los Angeles , CA 90014
Ph: (213) 627-5069
Em: ritagonzal@aol.com

Sonia Gonzalez
429 East 114 Street #8
New York, NY 10029

Laura Jacqueline Gonzalez-Carlos
MediaVision
3801 West Temple Avenue
Pomona, CA 91768
Ph: (909) 869-4762
Fx: (909) 869-3933
Em: jgonzalezcar@csupchncha.edu

Maureen T. Gosling
6540 Dana St.
Oakland , CA 94609
Ph: (510) 595-7926
Fx: (510 525 1204
Em: mgosling@aol.com

Adam Gottlieb
California Arts Council
1300 I St. Suite 930
Sacramento, CA 95814
Ph: (916) 322-6588
Fx: (916) 322-6575
Em: agottlieb@caartscouncil.com

Evangeline E. "Vangie" Griego
About Time Productions
3397 Cazador St.
Los Angeles, CA 90065
Ph: (323) 221-2180
Fx: (323) 221-1763
Em: Abouttyme@aol.com

Roberto Guerra
41 West 28th St.
New York , NY 10001

Noel Guglielmi
13931 Chadron Ave. # 5
Hawthorn , CA 90250
Ph: (310) 676-0578

172

Juan Guillen
Mano a Mano Productions
211 Cleveland St.
Brooklyn, NY 11208

Luis Guizar
5653 Rangeview Ave C
Los Angeles , CA 90042
Ph: (323) 257-4003

Charlotte Gutierrez
Cine Acción
346 9th Street
San Francisco, CA 94103-3809
Ph: (415) 553-8135
Fx: (415) 553-8137
Em: CineAccion@aol.com

Vincent A. Gutierrez
Aizada Productions
16354 Community St.
North Hills, CA 91343
Ph: (818) 895-0639
Fx: (818) 895-9433
Em: vincent.gutierrez@csun.edu

Michelle Habell-Pallan
University of Washington
4705 16th Ave NE
Seattle, WA 98105
Ph: (206) 522-2880
Fx: (206) 616-4071
Em: mhabellp@u.washington.edu

Sonia Hagler
PO Box 22836
Little Rock, AR 72221
Ph: (501) 666- 4522(501) 258-6561

John Hanhardt
Guggenheim Museum
575 Broadway
New York, NY 10012

Cheryl Head
Project Dev. Officer
Corporation for Public Broadcasting
901 E Street NW
Washington, DC 20004-2037
Ph: (202) 879-9682
Em: CHead@cpb.org

Patricia A. Heisser-Metoyer
Affirmative Action
Screen Actors Guild
5757 Wilshire Blvd.
Los Angeles, CA 90036-3600
Ph: (323) 549-6643
Fx: (323) 549-6647

Bel Hernandez
LatinHeat
146 N. San Fernando Blvd. #201
Burbank, CA 91502
Ph: (818) 846-9259
Fx: (818) 846-9419
Em: bel@latinheat.com

Dan Hernandez
P.O. Box 90
Montebello , CA 90640
Ph: (562) 439-6901
Fx: (562) 856-8941

Peggy Hernandez
Queen of Hearts Productions
227 Glenwood Ave.
San Jose, CA 95125
Ph: (408) 298-2724
Em: peggy_hernandez@msn.com

Francisco Hernández
El Norte Productions
8701 West Olympic Blvd
Los Angeles, CA 90035
Ph: (310) 360-1194
Fx: (310) 360-1199

Robert Hess
155 West 72nd St. #404
New York , NY 10023
Ph: (212) 579-0689

Robin Hickman
622 Oakdale Ave.
St. Paul, MN 55107

Ted Hope
Good Machine Inc.
417 Canal Street
New York, NY 10013

Cristina Ibarra
611 Broadway Suite 616
New York , NY 10012

Rich Islas
Pegasus Productions
124 Roma Ave.
Buffalo, NY 14215
Ph: (716) 893-0206

Rudy Jaimes
50 Horatio Street #19
New York , NY 10014
Ph: (212) 691-9260
Em: xwoox@earthlink.net

Al Jerome
President & CEO
KCET
4401 Sunset Blvd.
Los Angeles, CA 90027
Ph: (323) 953-5320
Fx: (323) 953-5347
Em: ajerome@kcet.org

Jennifer Jimenez
An Eagle Tribute Productions
11734 Wilshire Blvd.
Los Angeles, CA 90025
Ph: (310) 915-3072
Fx: (310) 268-9107
Em: jorgej9@gte.net

Jorge Jimenez
An Eagle Tribute Productions
11734 Wilshire Blvd.
Los Angeles, CA 90025
Ph: (310) 915-3072
Fx: (310) 268-9107
Em: jorgej9@gte.net

John Alexander Jiménez
5370 64th St.
Sacramento , CA 95820
Ph: (916) 455-0143
Fx: (916) 455-0143
Em: jiminez@softcom.net

Lillian Jiménez
One Donna Street
New City , NY 10956
Ph: (914) 634-5251
Fx: (914) 634-5251
Em: Lilpiri@aol.com

Lana Johnson
3115 Fremont Ave. S. #2
Minneapolis , MN 55408
Ph: (612) 821-0942
Em: clay_covered@yahoo.com

Jackie Kain
KCET-TV
4401 Sunset Blvd
Los Angeles, CA 90027
Ph: (323) 953-5259
Em: jkain@kcet.org

Gary D. Keller
Arizona State University
Hispanic Research Center 872702
Tempe, AZ 85257-2702
Ph: (602) 965-3990
Fx: (602) 965-0315
Em: gary.keller@asu.edu

Miguel Kohan
K Productions
11910 Weddington St. #304
North Hills, CA 91607
Ph: (310) 266-8075
Fx: (818) 509-1165
Em: kfilm@earthlink.net

Lili Kristan
ManJon Productions
5601 Bandera Road Ste. 410
San Antonio, TX 78238
Ph: (210) 523-7748
Fx: (210) 523-2696
Em: lili@manjon.com

Leslie LaPage
Infinity Films
P.O. Box 2632
Toluca Lake, CA 91610
Ph: (213) 387-3877
Fx: (213) 387-3808
Em: infinityfilm@earthlink.net

Terry Lawler
Women in Film
6 East 39th Street
New York, NY 10016

Ruby Lerner
Creative Capital
65 Bleecker Street
New York, NY 10012

Diane Librizzi
La Loca Entertainment, Inc
50 Webster Ave
New Rochelle, NY 10801
Em: Latmedia@aol.com

Mark Lloyd
Civil Rights Forum
818 18th Street NW Suite 505
Washington, DC 20006
Ph: (202) 887-0301
Fx: (202) 887-0305
Em: mlloyd@civilrightsforum.org

Cynthia López
79-10 34th Ave. #3-1
Jackson Heights , NY 11372
Ph: (212) 989.8121
Fx: (212) 989.8230
Em: Clopez@pov.org

Maria Lozano
8995 Keith Ave #9
West Hollywood , CA 90069
Ph: (310) 274-3197
Fx: (310) 274-3298
Em: melozano1@aol.com

Alfred Lugo
12902 Helmer Drive
Whittier , CA 90602
Ph: (562) 696-6204
Fx: (714) 895-0811
Em: alugo@koce.ccc.edu

David Maciel
Fulbright Program/American
Embassy
P.O. Box 3087
Laredo, TX 78044-3087
Em: dmaciel@dis1.cide.mx

Tony Magaña
811 N. Lopez Ave.
Los Angeles , CA 90022
Ph: (323) 263-1305
Em: tmagana@aya.yale.edu

Veronica Majano
336 Hanover Avenue
Oakland , CA 94606
Ph: (510) 452-8582
Em: v.majano@yahoo.com

Victoria M Maldonado
Cooper Station
PO Box 1165
New York, NY 10276

Sonia Malfa
40 Cottage St.
Buffalo , NY 14201
Ph: (716) 881-9094
Em: malf@acsu.buffalo.edu

Diana Manecchia
Latino Public Broadcasting
FASE
4801 Wilshire Blvd. #215
Los Angeles, CA 90010
Ph: (323) 937-9911
Em: diana.manecchia@fasenet.org

Robert Martin
Edge Productions
870 Market Street Suite 767
San Francisco, CA 94102
Ph: (415) 781-3343
Fx: (415) 781-3343
Em: edgecinema@aol.com

Alma R. Martinez
Stanford University
P.O. Box 8986
Stanford, CA 94309
Ph: (650) 329-9763
Fx: (650) 328-5155
Em: bneducda@.e.and.stanford.edu

Yvette María Martinez
Television Race Initiative
2601 Mariposa St. 3rd floor
San Francisco, CA 94110
Ph: (415) 553-2841
Fx: (415) 553-2848
Em: highimpacttv@pov.org

Margarita Martinez Cannon
R. Montalban New Film.
C/o Raleigh Studios
650 N. Bronson Suite 102
Hollywood, CA 90004
Ph: (323) 466-1156
Fx: (323) 466-8540

Bienvenida Matías
Center for Arts Criticism
2822 Lyndale Avenue S.
Minneapolis, MN 55408
Ph: (612) 874-2819
Fx: (612) 871-6927
Em: cac@intermediaarts.org

Luis Matías
IF-MC-CA-DI
1840 Grand Concourse
Bronx, NY 10457
Ph: (718) 466-1000
Fx: (718) 466-1220

Tomas Matteus
999 Irene Court
Valley Stream , NY 11580

Jesus Cantu Medel
Cine Cuahtemoc Pan American
314 Cosmos
Houston, TX 77009
Ph: (713) 223-2783

Alberto Medina
729 El Camino Real #102
Burlingame , CA 94010
Ph: (650) 548-0805
Em: mexotic@pacbell.net

Sergio Mendez
Giselle's
1601 University Ave.
Riverside, CA 92501
Ph: (909) 274-9247
Fx: (909) 274-9245
Em: gisellesmodels@earthlink.net

Jim Mendiola
226 Wickes Street
San Antonio , TX 78210
Ph: (210) 223-2625
Em: hidalgo12@aol.com

Robert Mendoza
800 35th St.
Richmond , CA 94805
Ph: (510) 236-2595
Em: robert_mendoza@umit.maine.edu

Juan Menzor-Rivera
1514 Alice St. #24
Oakland , CA 94612
Ph: (501) 628-0601
Fx: (415) 978-9635

Cara Mertes
POV
220 West 19th St
New York, NY 10011
Ph: (212) 989.8121
Fx: (212) 989.8230
Em: Cmertes@pov.org

Deana Mesa
7 Jane Street 3F
New York , NY 10014

Nestor Miranda
Mra Productions
44-45 21st. St. 3rd Fl.
Long Island City, NY 11101
Ph: (718) 391-0217
Fx: (718) 472-2966
Em: nesndi@yahoo.com

Karin Morales
Online Content Producer: El Sitio
USA
311 Lincoln Rd. # 204
Miami Beach, FL 33139
Ph: (305) 428-5116
Fx: (305) 428-5135
Em: kmorales@elsitioinc.net

Robert Morales
DeAnza College
661 Hermitage Way
San Jose, CA 95134
Ph: (408) 944-9558
Fx: (408) 944-9558
Em: darktangos@hotmail.com

Rosa Erendira Morales
Red Rosa Communications
5 Roethke Court
Saginaw, MI 48602
Ph: (517) 790-7353
Fx: (517) 797-8061
Em: redrosa@aol.com

Juan Moran
KQED Center for Education
2601 Mariposa St.
San Francisco, CA 94110-1400
Ph: (415) 553-2265
Fx: (415) 553-2456
Em: jmoran@kqed.org

Bill Moreno
41 Sutter St. #1200
San Francisco , CA 94104
Ph: (415) 841-9990
Fx: (415) 585-3414

Carmencristina Moreno
624 E. Carrillo Ave.
Fresno , CA 93725-9522
Ph: (559) 834-1407
Fx: (559) 834-5742
Em: carmencristina@att.net

Dorinda Moreno
Hitec Aztec Communications Network
76 Adobe Dr.
Concord, CA 94520
Ph: (925) 676-6241
Em: dorinda@pacbell.net

Mylene Moreno
Souvenir Pictures
7924 Hillside Ave.
Los Angeles, CA 90046
Ph: (323) 512-4678
Fx: (323) 512-4679
Em: mylenem@earthlink.net

Hillary Morgan
Pacific Islanders in Communications
1221 Kapoolani Suite 6A-4
Honolulu, HI 96814
Ph: (808) 591-0059
Fx: (808) 591-1114

Ann Moriyasu
Pacific Islanders in Communications
1221 Kapoolani Suite 6A-4
Honolulu, HI 96814
Ph: (808) 591-0059
Fx: (808) 591-1114

Marcela Moya
292 Palmer Street #A2
Costa Mesa , CA 92627
Ph: (949) 646-8908
Em: marcela5@hotmail.com

Juan Miguel Muniz
CNN
6430 Sunset Blvd. # 300
Los Angeles, CA 90028
Ph: (323) 993-5042
Fx: (323) 993-5188
Em: juan.muniz@turner.com

Alyce Myatt
John T. & Catherine D. MacArthur Fnd
140 South Dearborn Street #1100
Chicago, IL 60603-6285
Ph: (310) 360-1194
Fx: (310) 360-1199

Gregory Nava
El Norte Productions
8701 West Olympic Blvd
Los Angeles, CA 90035
Ph: (310) 360-1194
Fx: (310) 360-1199

Lisa Navarrete
National Council of La Raza
1111 19th St. NW
Washington, DC 20036
Ph: (202) 785-1670
Fx: (202) 776-1792
Em: lnavarrete@nclr.org

Jesus Nebot
ZOKALO
710 Adelaide Place
Santa Monica , CA 90402
Ph: (310) 393-1066
Fx: (310) 393-7764
Em: jesusnebot@earthlink.com

Frances Negrón-Muntaner
Polyamorphous Pictures
5 Island Ave. 11K
Miami Beach, FL 33139
Ph: (305) 672-0322
Fx: (305) 673-1665
Em: bikbaporub@aol.com

Diane Nelson
KQED
2601 Mariposa
San Francisco, CA 94110
Ph: (415) 553-2298
Em: dnelson@kqed.org

Kathleen Newman
Spanish & Portuguese Dept.
University of Iowa
111 Phillips Hall
Iowa City, IA 55242
Ph: (319) 335-1823
Fx: (319) 335-2990
Em: kathleen-newman@uiowa.edu

Gustavo Nieto
Television Services
7230 N.W. 58th St.
Miami, FL 33166
Ph: (305) 436-1159
Fx: (305) 433-0974
Em: gustavo@centauro.com

Leticia Nieto
1367 Bigalow Ave. NE
Olympia , WA 98506
Ph: (360) 754-6053
Fx: (360) 709-9659
Em: cuetzpalin@aol.com

Yvette Nieves Cruz
42 Park Avenue
New Rochelle , NY 10805
Em: Yvette_Nieves@elob.org

Alex Nogales
National Hispanic Media Coalition
2514 S. Grand Avenue
Los Angeles, CA 90007
Ph: (213) 746-6988
Fx: (213) 746-1305

Chon A. Noriega
UCLA Film & Television
102 E. Melnitz
Los Angeles, CA 90095
Ph: (310) 825-7061
Fx: (310) 825-3383
Em: cnoriega@ucla.edu

Louisa Novelo
Nosotros
650 N. Bronson Ave # 102
Hollywood, CA 90078
Ph: (323) 466-1156
Fx: (323) 466-8540
Em: brysonvega@aol.com

Euripides Nuñez
12025 Hoffman St.
Studio City , CA 91604
Ph: (818) 980-8763
Fx: (818) 980-8763

Antonio "Bogey" Olivas III
Bailando Pictures
Future Artists Network
1167 N. Hobart Blvd. #8
Los Angeles, CA 90029
Ph: (213) 460-4616
Em: future_artists@hotmail.com

Dorothy Olmos
Theatre on Broadway
Assoc. of Hispanic Fine Arts
420 Broadway St.
Houston, TX 77012-1708
Ph: (713) 928-3538
Fx: (713) 928-2688

Edward J. Olmos
Latino Public Broadcasting
6777 Hollywood Blvd. # 500
Los Angeles, CA 90028
Ph: (323) 466-7110
Fx: (323) 466-7521

Paulette Orona
8651 Wonderland Ave.
Los Angeles , CA 91343
Ph: (323) 656-2408

Roberta Orona-Cordova
CSUN and Alzada Productions
16354 Community St.
North Hills, CA 91343
Ph: (818) 895-0639
Fx: (818) 985-9933
Em: roberta.orona@email.csun.edu

Raquel Ortiz
64 Read St. #2
Cambridge , MA 02140
Ph: (617) 262-8830
Fx: (617) 262-7432
Em: rortiz@vpg.com

Harry Pachon
Tomás Rivera Policy Institute
241 E. 11th St. Steele Hall
Claremont, CA 91711-6194
Ph: (909) 621-8897
Fx: (909) 621-8898
Em: harry.pachon@cgu.edu

Adriana E. Padilla
P.O. Box 10746
Beverly Hills , CA 90213
Ph: (323) 883-1600

Sandy Pedlow
Director Program Strategies
Corporation for Public Broadcasting
901 E Street NW
Washington, DC 20004-2037
Em: SPedlow@cpb.org

Jaime Pelayo
10170 Laurel Canyon Blvd.
Pacoima , CA 91331
Ph: (818) 219 4702
Fx: (310) 281-3770
Em: jaime@pacificnet.net

Dora & Manuel J. Peña
6838 Spring Garden
San Antonio , TX 78249
Ph: (210) 699-4338

Pocha Peña
Fox Latin America
725 S. Spring Loft 20
Los Angeles, CA 90014
Ph: (213) 627-8588
Fx: (323) 391-1490
Em: unapocha@hotmail.com

Jeff J. Penichet
Hispanic Film Project
/Penichet Productions
2514 S. Grand Ave.
Los Angeles, CA 90007
Ph: (213) 749-6213
Fx: (213) 749-1820
Em: filmdoer@aol.com

Onorio Perez
Manhattan Neighborhood Network
537 West 59th St.
New York, NY 10019

Dianna Pérez
Es Tiempo Productions
14945 Marquette Street
Moor Park, CA 93021
Ph: (805) 523-8011
Fx: (805) 523-8011

Sandra M. Pérez
AHA! Association of Hispanic Arts
250 West 26th St. 4th Fl.
New York, NY 10001
Ph: (212) 727-7227
Fx: (212) 727-0549
Em: aha96@aol.com

Severo Pérez
Script & Post Script
PO Box 26407
Los Angeles, CA 90026
Ph: (323) 662-0265
Fx: (323) 662-2249
Em: spfilms@aol.com

Maria Perez Brown
Dorado Entertainment Inc.
1633 Broadway
New York, NY 10019

Luis Pérez-Tolón
Discovery Networks
Latin America/Iberia
6505 Blue Lagoon Dr. # 300
Miami, FL 33126
Ph: (305) 461-4710
Em: Luis_Perez_Tolon@discovery.com

Rafael Pérez-Torres
234 West Figueroa St.
Santa Barbara , CA 93101
Ph: (805) 966-1165
Fx: (805) 966-2154
Em: perezt@humnet.ucla.edu

Elizabeth Peters
AIVF
304 Hudson St. 6th Fl.
New York, NY 10013
Ph: (212) 807-1400
Fx: (212) 463-8519
Em: elizabeth@aivf.org

Miren Petrikorena
15309 Germain St.
Mission Hill , CA 91345

Julia Pimsleur
Big Mouth Productions
443 Broadway 5th Fl.
New York, NY 10013
Ph: (212) 343-9606
Fx: (212) 343-2609
Em: big-mouth-
prod@mindspring.com

Karen Plount
Communications Council
Nielsen Media Research
1627 K St. NW
Washington , DC 20006
Ph: (202) 296-1936
Fx: (202) 296-7906
Em: arnolde@tvratings.com

Lourdes Portillo
Xochill Film and Video
981 Esmeralda St.
San Francisco, CA 94110
Ph: (415) 642-1614
Fx: (415) 642-1609
Em: portillo@sirius.com

Michael Pryfogle
190 Tiffany Ave.
San Francisco , CA 94110
Ph: (415) 826-8254
Fx: (415) 821-6220
Em: terrapin@sirius.com

Georgia Quiñones
Sologaistoa
19389 Hidden Valley Road
Guerneville, CA 95446
Ph: (707) 869-1435
Fx: (707) 869-9785
Em: dbell@pacbell.net

Rogelio Domingo Quiñones
RQ Productions
1017 E. California
El Paso, TX 79902-4620
Ph: (915) 533-3254
Fx: (915) 533-3254

Ernesto Quintero
4 Brown Hats
3577 Griffin Ave.
Los Angeles, CA 90031
Ph: (213) 225-2919
Fx: (213) 225-1353
Em: fbrownhats@aol.com

Susan Racho
914 Wilson Ave #5
Glendale , CA 91206
Ph: (818) 551-9619
Fx: (818) 551-9619
Em: sracho@aol.com

Victoria & Joe Ramiréz
120 Maple Street
Crookston , MN 56716
Ph: (218) 281-2130

Anna Ramos
WNET
450 W. 33rd St.
New York, NY 10001

Karen Ranucci
Latin American Video Archives
124 Washington Place
New York, NY 10014

Stephanie Rauber
Rauber Filmworks
530 E. 13th St. #10
New York, NY 10019
Ph: (212) 529-9711
Fx: (212) 253-5310

Ruben Reyes
2860 W. Desert Crest Drive
Tucson , AZ 85713
Ph: (520) 624-7313
Fx: (520) 884-1152
Em: rreyes@exchange.co.pima.az.us

Javier Reyna
P.O. Box 2701
Blue Jay , CA 92317
Ph: (909) 336-2662
Fx: (909) 336-1171
Em: sajav@prodigy.net

Frank Richards
Action Talent Management
6255 Sunset Blvd. Suite 2201
Los Angeles, CA 90028
Ph: (323) 461-5155
Fx: (323) 461-5855
Em: frank@actiontalent.com

Dr. Diana Rios
Dept. Comm. Sciences U-85
University of Connecticut
Storrs, CT 06269
Ph: (860) 486-3187
Fx: (860) 486-2906
Em: drios@uconnvm.uconn.edu

Alex Rivera
611 Broadway Suite 616
New York , NY 10012
Ph: (212) 253-6273
Fx: (212) 253-6284
Em: arivera@interport.net

Cathy Rivera
21007 Van Deene Ave.
Torrance , CA 90502-1741
Ph: (310) 475-2230
Fx: (310) 475-2089
Em: criticsriv@aol.com

Jonathan Robinson
When in Doubt Productions
3608 19th St.
San Francisco, CA 94110
Ph: (415) 487-2652
Fx: (415) 626-7586
Em: jmrsf@yahoo.com

Baldemar Rodriguez
605 Brown Dr.
Pasadena , TX 77506
Ph: (713) 477-9446
Fx: (713) 477-9446
Em: baldemarrodriguez@latino.com

Eugene Rodriguez
Illumination Productions
1106-B Valencia Street
San Francisco, CA 94110
Ph: (415) 647-6217
Em: ear7581@mercury.fhda.edu

Isaías D. Rodriguez
Pacific News Service
660 Market #210
San Francisco, CA 94104
Ph: (415) 438-4755
Fx: (415) 438-4935
Em: irodriguez@pacificnews.org

Joe Rodriguez
Sunstone Pictures
12128 Pantheon Street
Norwalk , CA 90605
Ph: (626) 546-9494
Em: joerodriguez@earthlink.net

Maria Teresa Rodriguez
1320 Alder St.
Philadelphia , PA 19147
Ph: (215) 467-4417
Fx: (215) 898-9804
Em: marite001@aol.com

Phillip Rodriguez
921 ½ Micheltorena St.
Los Angeles , CA 90026
Ph: (323) 661-5705
Fx: (323) 661-5608
Em: ba433@lafn.org

Robert Israel Rodriguez
San Pedro Springs:
A Motion Picture Company
162 Harrigan Ct. #3 / P.O. 6889
San Antonio, TX 78209
Ph: (210) 824-8468

Rafael P. Román
WNET
450 W. 33rd St.
New York, NY 10001
Ph: (212) 560-4948
Em: proman@wnet.org

Pedro Romero
1838 Chestnut St.
Oakland , CA 94607-2787

Sonia Rosario
9 North Moore St.
New York , NY 10013
Ph: (212) 588-9447
Fx: (212) 588-0708
Em: sonia_rosario@wgbh.org

Adriana Rosas-Walsh
Cine Acción/
Film Arts Foundation
346 Ninth St. 2nd Fl.
San Francisco, CA 94103
Ph: (415) 552-8760
Fx: (415) 552-0882
Em: adrianarw@filmarts.org

Robert Rose
Artist and Idea Management
1 Astor Place 5S
New York, NY 10003
Ph: (212) 253-6153
Fx: (212) 253-7007
Em: Rob@ArtistAndIdea.com

Benjamin Rosen
128 Madison Avenue #2RS
New York , NY 10016

Michael Ruiz
Aerospace Engineer
Aeroscience & Flight Mechanics Div.
NASA-Johnson Space Center, EG2
Houston, TX 77058
Ph: (281) 483-8169
Fx: (281) 483-1245

Citlali Sáenz
Radio Bilingüe
Fort Mason Center Bldg D # 210
San Francisco, CA 94123
Ph: (415) 674-0926
Fx: (415) 771-5466

Richard Saiz
Production Manager
ITVS
51 Federal St.
San Francisco, CA 94107
Ph: (415) 356-8383
Em: richard_saiz@itvs.pbs.org

Carlos San Miguel
2335 Glover Pl.
Los Angeles, CA 90031
Ph: (323) 276-5932
Em: latinoactor @ hotmail.com

David J. Sanchez
Long Beach Pictures
3052 Wynwood Lane #4
Los Angeles, CA 90023
Ph: (323) 263-3352

Felix Sanchez
Natl Hispanic Fdn. for the Arts
Waterfront Center
1010 Wisconsin Ave. NW # 210
Washington , DC 20007
Ph: (202) 293-8330
Fx: (202) 965-5252
Em: www.HispanicArts.org

Josef Sanchez
NLCC
P.O. Box 33301
Los Angeles, CA 90033
Ph: (323) 980-1075
Fx: (323) 663-5606
Em: jasanchez@pacbell.net

Joshua Sanchez
Latino USA
University of Texas
Communication Bldg. B Rm 3142
Austin, TX 78712
Ph: (512) 471-2137
Fx: (512) 471-3700
Em: jsquash@mail.utexas.edu

Annette Sandoval
1240 Regent Street
Alameda , CA 94501
Ph: (510) 522-3240
Fx: (510) 323-9558
Em: sandoval@a.crl.com

Dario Sanmiguel
Archangel Films
1460 Haight St.
San Francisco, CA 94117
Ph: (415) 255-8723
Fx: (415) 255-8723
Em: dariodirdp@earthlink.net

Ray Santisteban
Guadalupe Cultural Arts Center
1300 Guadalupe Street
San Antonio, TX 78207
Ph: (210) 271-3151
Fx: (210) 271-3480
Em: rays@guadalupeculturalarts.org

Bernadine A. Santistevan
Santistevan Productions
1173A 2nd Avenue #183
New York, NY 10021
Ph: (212) 588-0126
Fx: (212) 588-0129
Em: bernadines@worldnet.att.net

John Phillip Santos
The Ford Foundation
320 East 43rd St.
New York, NY 10017
Ph: (212) 573-4914
Fx: (212) 351-3649
Em: j.santos@fordfound.org

Aurora Sarabiz
P.O. Box 13787
Berkeley , CA 94701

Ellen Schneider
P.O.V.
220 West 19th St. 11th Fl.
New York, NY 10011
Ph: (212) 989.8121
Fx: (212) 989.8230
Em: Ellen@pov.org

Margot Segura
Hispanic Education and Media Group
P.O. Box 221
Sausalito, CA 94966
Ph: (415) 331-8560
Fx: (415) 331-2636

Joan Shigekawa
Creativity & Cultural Division
The Rockefeller Foundation
420 Fifth Ave.
New York, NY 10018-2702

Gail Silva
Film Arts Foundation
346 9th St. 2nd Floor
San Francisco, CA 94117
Ph: (415) 552-8760
Fx: (415) 552-0882
Em: gails@jilmarts.org

Debbie Silverfine
NY State Council on the Arts
915 Broadway 8th fl.
New York, NY 10010

Connie Simonelli
3417 W. Drummond Pl. #1B
Chicago, IL 60647
Ph: (773) 665-7305
Em: cjsimone@msn.com

Enrique Soberanes
472 Via Mira Monte
Montebello , CA 90640

Helena Solberg
200 West 90th Street
New York NY, 10024

Irene Sosa
239 3rd Street
Jersey City , NJ 07302

Bea Stotzer
303 South Loma Drive
Los Angeles , CA 90017
Ph: (323) 663-8294
Fx: (323) 663-5606
Em: email4new@aol.com

Otto "Tito" Stürcke
Rebel Arte – Art of a Nation
8556 Robert Ave.
Sun Valley , CA 91352
Ph: (818) 875-5682
Em: Rebelarte@aol.com

David Sweet-Cordero
Intercultura Bilingual Media
513 Valencia Suite 10
San Francisco, CA 94110
Ph: (415) 648-8723
Fx: (415) 642-4689
Em: dscordero@intercultura.com

Lauren Tamara
El Tecolote
1850 Union St. #1580
San Francisco, CA 94123
Ph: (415) 351-1113
Em: ltamara@ipost.net

Taina TV Productions
604 Tompkins Ave. #D6
Mamaroneck, NY 10543

Lauri R. Tanner
Film Festival Consultants
337 Nevada Street
San Francisco, CA 94110-6106
Ph: (415) 550-9445
Fx: (415) 824-5118
Em: laurirose@aol.com

Rick Tejada Flores
Paradigm Productions
1250 Addison
Berkeley, CA 94702
Ph: (510) 883-9814
Fx: (510) 843-0138
Em: grtf@paradigmproductions.org

Ray Telles
Paradigm Productions
1250 Addison
Berkeley, CA 94702
Ph: (510) 883-9814
Fx: (510) 843-0138
Em: Rto2900@aol.com

Max R. Terronez
UC Santa Cruz
Exposure Plus
1225 17th Ave. #28
Santa Cruz, CA 95062
Ph: (831) 476-6066
Em: mterronez@aol.com

Fabiola Torres
CSUN
21811 Nordhoff Street
North Ridge, CA 91330
Ph: (818) 677-2824
Fx: (818) 677-7578
Em: fabiola.torres@csun.edu

Robert Torres
502 West 141 St. #5A
New York , NY 10031

Maria Tototzintle
Twin Cities Public Television
172 East Fourth St.
St. Paul, MN 55101
Ph: (612) 222-1717
Em: mtototzintle@ktca.org

Joseph Tovares
The American Experience
WGBH
125 Western Avenue
Boston, MA 02134
Ph: (617) 492-2777
Fx: (617)254-7535
Em: joseph_tovares@wgbh.org

Carmelita Tropicana
15 Avenue C #1
New York , NY 10009
Ph: (212) 979-9225
Fx: (212) 979-0135
Em: atropix@aol.com

Ela Troyano
15 Avenue C
New York , NY 10009
Ph: (212) 979-0135
Fx: (212) 979-0135
Em: etroyano@aol.com

183

Joi Turner
Spirit Dance Entertainment
1023 N. Orange Drive
Los Angeles, CA 90038
Ph: (323) 512-7998
Fx: (323) 512-7996
Em: go4joi@earthlink.net

Pepe Urquijo
Bandido Productions
Xicano Records and Films
42 Rudden Avenue
San Francisco, CA 94112
Ph: (415) 560-5628
Fx: (415) 924-1142
Em: pepelicula@hotmail.com

John Valadez
Kitchen Sync
36 Oriole Way
Dix Hills, NY 11746
Ph: (516) 421-6931
Fx: (516) 421-6923
Em: valadezhsu@aol.com

Betty L. Valdés
Community Affairs Officer
Montgomery County Public Libraries
99 Maryland Avenue
Rockville, MD 20850
Ph: (240)777-0017
Fx: (240) 777-0014
Em: valdeb@co.mo.md.us

David Valdez
10 Jordan Avenue
Los Altos , CA 94022
Ph: (650) 949-3516
Em: homieknomes@yahoo.com

Rosalia Valencia
Cine Acción
346 Ninth St.
San Francisco, CA 94103
Ph: (415) 553-8135
Fx: (415) 553-8137
Em: cineaccion@aol.com

Jose Luis Valenzuela
Sleeping Giant Productions
5911 Allston St.
Los Angeles, CA 90022
Ph: (323) 887-0665
Fx: (323) 887-9600
Em: slgiant@aol.com

Isela Valenzuela Mendez
Giselle's
1601 University Ave.
Riverside, CA 92501
Ph: (909) 274-9247
Fx: (909) 274-9245
Em: gisellesmodels@earthlink.net

Domingo Vara
457 S. Ogden Drive
Los Angeles , CA 90036
Ph: (323)939-3715
Fx: (323)939-3715
Em: domingovara@hotmail.com

Willie Varela
UT at El Paso Theatre Arts
Fox Fine Arts #371
El Paso, TX 79968
Ph: (915) 747-7888
Fx: (915) 747-5438
Em: wvarela@utep.edu

Sandy Varga
Latin Heat
146 N. San Fernando Blvd. # 201
Burbank, CA 91502
Ph: (818) 846-9259
Fx: (818) 846-9419
Em: bel@latinheat.com

Regina Vater
4901 Caswell Ave
Austin, TX 78751
Ph: (512) 451-1674
Em: hydie@mail.utexas.edu

Gustavo Vazquez
787 Clayton Street #4
San Francisco , CA 94117
Ph: (415) 664-2712
Em: gustavov@exploratorium.edu

Luis A. Vazquez Gomez
Arroz Y Frijoles Productions
147 Madrid Street
San Francisco, CA 94110
Ph: (415) 587-7892
Em: luvasquez@aol.com

Carmen E. Vega
P.O. Box 20745
Los Angeles , CA 90006
Ph: (213) 694-2032
Fx: (213) 365-2449

Jerry G. Velasco
Nosotros Inc.
650 N. Bronson Ave. #102
Hollywood, CA 90004
Ph: (323) 466-8566
Fx: (323) 466-8540

Edín Velez
2840 Broadway #278
New York , NY 10025
Ph: (212) 477-0969
Em: edinvelez@aol.com

Ricardo J. Verdoni
Verdoni Productions
610 Lyon Street
Saginaw, MI 48602
Ph: (517) 792-2531
Fx: (517) 793-0026
Em: verdoni@worldnet.att.net

Victoria Vieira
Latino Film Festival
145 Prospect Avenue
Sausalito, CA 94965
Ph: (415) 331-2502
Fx: (415) 331-5572
Em: sperel@linex.com

Miguel Villafane
Luna Films
C/ Pereira Leal
586 Urban. Valencia
San Juan, PR 0923-1903
Ph: (780) 753-1881
Fx: (787) 765-9659
Em: jmv333@aol.com

Maria Christina Villaseñor
Guggenheim Museum
575 Broadway
New York, NY 10012

Laura Welsh
National Endowment for the Arts
1100 Pennsylvania Ave. NW
Washington, DC 20506
Ph: (202) 682-5738
Em: welshl@arts.endow.gov

Celeste Serna Williams
Cine Las Americas
2215 Post Road #2056
Austin, TX 78704

Mimi Wisnosky
Pacific Islanders in Communications
1221 Kapoolani Suite 6A-4
Honolulu, HI 96814
Ph: (808) 591-0059
Fx: (808) 591-1114

Juan Carlos Zaldivar
Nota Bene Productions
71 E. 3rd St. #9
New York, NY 10003
Ph: (212) 598-1049
Fx: (212) 598-1049
Em: jucamaza@aol.com

Ariel Zapata
1921 Hoyne Avenue
Chicago , IL 60647
Ph: (773) 486-7901
Fx: (312) 573-1233
Em: arielzapata@megsinet.net

Mario Zapp
Media Alliance
814 Mission St. # 205
San Francisco, CA 94103
Ph: (415) 546-6334
Fx: (415) 546-6218
Em: classes@media-alliance.org

Esteban Zul
620 South Ardmore Ave.
Los Angeles , CA 90005
Ph: (213) 487-3927
Fx: (213) 380-0378

Frank Zuñiga
South West Institute of Film and TV
500 Copper NW Suite 315
Albuquerque, NM 87102
Ph: (505) 764-9995
Fx: (505) 764-9997
Em: fzuniga@uswest.net

Pedro Zurita
Videoteca del Sur
84 East 3rd St. Suite 5A
New York, NY 10003-9253
Ph: (212) 674-5405
Fx: (212) 614-0464
Em: videlsur96@aol.com

Contributors

Louis DeSipio is an Associate Professor of Political Science and the Interim Director of the Latina/Latino Studies Program at the University of Illinois at Urban-Champaign. His research focuses on ethnic politics, particularly Latino politics, immigration and immigrant settlement, and public policy. He is the author of *Counting on the Latino Vote: Latinos as a New Electorate* (University Press of Virginia, 1996). He is also the author and editor of a six-volume series on Latino political values, attitudes, and behaviors. The most recent volume in the series is *Making Americans, Remaking America: Immigration and Immigrant Policy* (Westview Press, 1998) co-edited with Rodolfo O. de la Garza.

Rita Gonzalez is a video artist, writer, and independent curator who lives and works in Los Angeles. Her video work has been screened at festivals and museums internationally. Her collaborative curatorial effort Mexperimental Cinema, a sixty-year survey of experimental media arts in Mexico, has traveled to the Guggenheim Museum, Pacific Film Archives, Festival de Cortometrajes, Mexico D.F., and many other venues. Currently, Gonzalez is in the Critical Studies doctoral program in the Department of Film and Television at UCLA.

Frances Negrón-Muntaner is an award-winning filmmaker, writer, journalist, and cultural critic. She has directed several films, including *Bricando El Charco: Portrait of a Puerto Rican* (1994) and is the president of Polymorphous Pictures, Inc. Negrón-Muntaner has written for both popular and academic publications in the U.S. and abroad. Her books include *Shouting in a Whisper: Latino Poets in Philadelphia* (Chile: Asterión Press, 1994) and *Puerto Rican Jam: Essays On Culture and Politics* (with Ramón Grosfoguel, University of Minnesota Press, 1997). Her first collection of prose and poetry,

Anatomy of a Smile and Other Poems, is forthcoming from Third Woman Press (California) in 2000. She is the recipient of both the Rockefeller Film/Video Fellowship (1997) and the Pen Fellowship in the Arts (1993).

LETICIA NIETO is a psychotherapist, dramatist, and educator specializing in intercultural relations, anti-oppression, and creativity. She has worked as a trainer and educator since 1980 and is currently a faculty member at Saint Martin's College in Olympia, Washington. She has been active as a performer since 1978. She holds advanced degrees in clinical psychology and human development.

CHON A. NORIEGA is Associate Professor and Vice Chair in the UCLA Department of Film and Television. He is author of *Shot in America: Television, the State, and the Rise of Chicano Cinema* (University of Minnesota Press, 2000) and editor of six books on Latino media and visual culture. He is also editor of *Aztlán: A Journal of Chicano Studies.*

RODOLFO O. DE LA GARZA is vice-president for research at the Tomás Rivera Policy Institute and Mike Hogg Professor of Community Affairs in the Department of Government at the University of Texas. He has published extensively on issues related to the impact of language use on political knowledge and policy preferences.

HARRY P. PACHON is president of the Tomás Rivera Policy Institute and Kenan Professor of Political Studies at Pitzer College and Claremont Graduate University. The Tomás Rivera Policy Institute is a non-partisan non-profit research organization that focuses on issues of concern to the nation's Hispanic community.

CHARLES RAMÍREZ BERG is University Distinguished Teaching Professor in film studies in the Department of Radio-Television-Film at the University of Texas at Austin. He is the author of two books on Mexican cinema and many articles on Latino images in Hollywood film. He is currently completing a book on Hollywood's Latino imagery entitled *Images and Counterimages* for the University of Texas Press.

JUAN JOSE RIVERA is a photographer, filmmaker, and videographer who resides in Oakland. Born in El Salvador, Rivera grew up in Los Angeles and studied film at UC Berkeley. He has also created multimedia installations incorporating original video productions. Rivera is currently editing his documentary video on a Salvadoran family in San Francisco's Mission District.

RAY SANTISTEBAN is an award-winning documentary producer currently living in San Antonio. He co-produced *Passin' It On*, a one-hour documentary on the false imprisonment of New York Black Panther leader Dhoruba Bin Wahad, and was an associate producer on the four-hour PBS broadcast series *Chicano!: The History of the Mexican American Civil Rights Movement*. Since 1997, Santisteban has been the director of media arts at the Guadalupe Cultural Arts Center.

JULIA SEGROVE JAURIGUI is the former director of Cine Acción. A San Francisco-based filmmaker, she recently completed a short narrative film, "Routine Disturbances," and is currently developing a feature-length screenplay, "Red and White." She serves on the Activist Advised Grantmaking Panel for the Paul Robeson Fund for Independent Media.

FABIOLA TORRES is a chingona who produces Chicano theater in Los Angeles and teaches at California State University, Northridge, and Glendale Community College. She is an advocate for young Latino representation in the media.